Five Centuries of Japanese Kimono

ON THIS SLEEVE OF FONDEST DREAMS

The Art Institute of Chicago

MUSEUM STUDIES

VOLUME 18, NO. 1

The Art Institute of Chicago
MUSEUM STUDIES

VOLUME 18, NO. 1

Five Centuries of Japanese Kimono:
On This Sleeve of Fondest Dreams

Foreword

In one of his woodblock prints that portray women wearing fashionable garments, the eighteenth-century Japanese artist Isoda Koryūsai depicted a courtesan seated before two women attendants. They display for her a man's *haori*, an informal outer coat. The remarkable lining of this costume reveals the snow-capped peak of Mount Fuji rising above the clouds. As this print suggests, the full meaning of traditional Japanese costumes is frequently hidden from view, for the sacred image of Mount Fuji would be concealed if the *haori* were worn. The idea of a design within a design is central to Japanese costume-making, and is suggested further in Koryūsai's print by the profuse layers of the courtesan's garments. Koryūsai's print evokes other themes, as well—the use of sacred imagery in traditional costumes; the interplay between costume design and painting, drawing, and printmaking; and the role of high fashion in costume-making—all of which figure importantly in the design and production of traditional Japanese costumes.

Each of these themes is examined in this special number of *Museum Studies*, which provides the first comprehensive study of the Art Institute's most important Japanese costumes. This issue has been published in conjunction with the exhibition "Five Centuries of Japanese Kimono: On This Sleeve of Fondest Dreams," held at The Art Institute of Chicago from March 7 to June 7, 1992, in which the costumes were displayed together for the first time.

The majority of the costumes discussed in this issue and featured in the exhibition were designed for Nō theater—the traditional form of Japanese theater that developed under the auspices of the ruling class. Within the stylized and subtle staging of Nō drama, the actors' ornate costumes stand in contrast to the bare stage and are therefore charged with great meaning. Our authors refer often to the significance of costumes within Nō theater as they discuss the techniques and fabrics used in making the costumes, the glorification of silk-making in woodblock prints, and the costume design books used in the manufacture of such garments. What emerges from these essays is a full and varied portrait of a complex

and, to the Western world, little-understood aspect of Japanese art.

As Monica Bethe, a scholar at the Kyoto Center for Japanese Studies, explains in her essay, costumes have long functioned as part of an intricate web of symbolism and allusion in Nō drama. The imagery of a Nō costume evokes the particular spirit and qualities of a character; in many instances, a costume design will use symbols and references from the Nō play being presented onstage. With Nō costumes as her focal point, Bethe has written a fascinating introduction to Nō theater.

In our second essay, scholars Mary and Ralph Hays provide a detailed analysis of the costumes in this issue based on their research and examination of the garments. The Hayses begin with an aesthetic and historical overview of Japanese costume-making before shifting to their main focus: the technical aspects of the Art Institute's most important Japanese costumes. Their essay examines closely the fabrics, dyes, and techniques utilized in the making of these costumes, as well as their historical context. In addition, the Hayses have contributed an extensive catalogue and a glossary.

Silk, of course, is the main component of Japanese costumes, and its manufacture—known as sericulture—has been revered traditionally by Japanese culture. Art Institute curator James Ulak, one of the organizers of the exhibition, has contributed an essay on a wonderful series of twelve prints by the famed printmaker Kitagawa Utamaro (1753–1806) that depicts the complete process of making silk. Utamaro's sericulture series, as Ulak explains in his lucid essay, combines a technically accurate depiction of silk-making with a voyeuristic portrayal of courtesans. The essay explores this seemingly odd juxtaposition, and it also provides a rich historical context for Utamaro's prints, tracing the graphic depiction of silk-making from the earliest known examples to Utamaro's time.

In our final article, Betty Siffert of the Department of Asian Art has assembled a portfolio of Japanese costume design books (*hinagata bon*) drawn from the collection of the Art Institute. Siffert discusses the history of this collection in her preface and explains the purpose of these volumes. As the reproductions and accompanying captions reveal, *hinagata bon* have traditionally provided costume designers with a wide range of ideas for the shape and ornamentation of their garments. The concerns of artists, artisans, merchants, and consumers come together in *hinagata bon*, and they provide a fitting conclusion to our examination of traditional Japanese costumes.

✻   ✻   ✻   ✻   ✻

The idea for this issue of *Museum Studies* was suggested by James N. Wood, President and Director of the Art Institute. We are grateful to him and the co-organizers of the exhibition, Christa C. Thurman, Curator of Textiles, and James Ulak, Associate Curator of Japanese Art. I would also like to thank a number of people at the Art Institute for assisting in the preparation of this issue of *Museum Studies*: Eva-Maria J. Schuchardt, Nina Weber, Susan Hammond, Cynthia J. Castañeda, and Michele H. Wright of the Department of Textiles; Mary Albert and Jamyn Flynn of the Department of Asian Art; Leslie Umberger and Pam Stuedemann of the Department of Imaging and Technical Services; and Susan F. Rossen, Elisabeth Dunn, Cris Ligenza, and Bryan Miller of the Publications Department. I am also grateful to Robert V. Sharp and Katherine Houck Fredrickson of the Publications Department and Ann Gross of the Department of Graphic Services for their invaluable contributions. Finally, I would like to express particular appreciation to Lorna Ann Filippini, Associate Conservator in the Department of Textiles; Nancy K. Finn, also of the Department of Textiles, who photographed all of the museum's costumes reproduced in this issue; and Betty Siffert of the Department of Asian Art for their unstinting efforts in making possible this issue of *Museum Studies*.

MICHAEL SITTENFELD
Editor

Isoda Koryūsai (Japanese, active 1766–1788). *Oiran Hayama no Asahimaru-ya (Courtesan Hayama of Sunrise House)*, c. 1778. From the series *Hinagata Wakana no Hatsu Moyō* (*New Designs as Fresh as Young Leaves*). Woodblock print; 38.4 x 25.8 cm. The Art Institute of Chicago, Clarence Buckingham Collection of Japanese Prints (1925.2223).

The Use of Costumes in Nō Drama

MONICA BETHE

Kyoto Center for Japanese Studies

The rich gorgeous brocades, embroidered satins, and diaphanous glittering gauzes that are labeled "Nō costume" in a museum were originally intended to be draped in layers over an actor, molding him into the image of a role. Elaborate rules determine the types of garments to be worn for the roles of soldier or woodsman, heavenly maiden or wrathful god, playful lion or menacing demon. Although social station dictates that courtiers wear the ankle-bound pantaloons of the nobility (*sashinuki*), and priests a simple traveling cloak, in general the costumes make little attempt to be realistic. For example, the lowly girls collecting brine for salt-making wear richly embroidered robes sparkling with gold leaf. In addition to designating a role, the costumes are meant to evoke the atmosphere of the play, functioning much like a stage set in Western theater. Since the plain wooden stage of the Nō theater remains unadorned, costumes are the primary focus of visual interest. The patterns of the costumes suggest season and setting, often echoing verbal imagery central to the play, while their colors evoke mood and suggest sensibility.

Nō drama began as folk theater performed as part of religious ceremonies. But under the patronage of the shogunate, Nō theater from the middle of the fourteenth century onward developed into a highly refined poetic theater centered on music and dance. During the Edo period (1603–1868), Nō was the official entertainment of the shogunate court and was performed at state functions. Both the shogun and regional lords, *daimyo*, patronized actor troupes, and competed in accumulating the finest masks and costumes. The official role of the shogunate in the growth of Nō drama, as well as the patronage of the upper class, contrasts with the role of the

middle class in the rise of Kabuki, which developed in the entertainment districts of Osaka, Kyoto, and Edo during the seventeenth century. While Kabuki aggrandizes the drama of life in society with elaborate sets, exaggerated makeup, and flashy costumes, Nō intensifies the vision of the spirit with a single painted pine as a constant "set," with subtle masks, and with conservatively magnificent costumes. Internalized, understated, and very refined, the Nō performance is a well-wrought poem in which imagistic integrity overshadows plot. The costumes function within the tightly intertwined poetic fiber. Not only is the patterning on the costumes a visual poetry in itself, but references to costuming elaborate the poetry, and the visual impact of the costumes supports and underscores the words of the text.

The uses of costume as they appear in the texts are many-leveled. Costumes can serve as identification cards, or precipitate the fusion of personalities. Other uses reflect Japanese social customs of the period when Nō drama developed. At that time, cloth and clothing were customary payments and presents. The textual enumera-

FIGURE 1. Tsukioka Kogyo (Japanese, 1869–1927). *Aoinue*, early twentieth century. Print no. 11 from the series *Nōgaku hyakuban* (vol. 2). Woodblock print; 25.9 x 38 cm. The Art Institute of Chicago, Bequest of Henry C. Schwab Estate (1943.834). In this scene from the Nō play *Aoinue*, the spirit of Lady Rokujo menaces the ailing Aoi, who is represented by a kimono laid on the stage. The pattern of triangles on Rokujo's upper kimono (*surihaku*) represents scales and are intended to suggest her serpentine — and evil — nature, which can also be detected in her horned, gnashing mask. Rokujo's dark-ground *nuihaku* is worn as skirts in *koshimaki* style over the *surihaku*, and is similar in its ornamentation to a *nuihaku* in the Art Institute's collection (see pl. 5; cat. no. 3).

tion of the attire of a character, which is not necessarily identical with the actual costume worn, stems from a concern with dress as a statement of rank and personality, a concern that runs through much of Japanese literature and reflects long-standing attitudes of society. In many plays, articles of clothing—a robe, hat, or cloak—also function as props. They are draped over an object, placed onstage, or handed from actor to actor. The action surrounding a garment is often central to the unfolding of a play.

Costume as Identity

Perhaps the most striking example of the ingenious use of costume as a prop appears in the play *Aoinoue*. The ailing wife of Hikaru Genji, Lady Aoi, is haunted by the menacing, jealous spirit of one of Genji's lady loves, Rokujo Miyasudokoro. Throughout the play, Aoi lies prostrate and immobilized on the stage, represented by a *kosode*-style robe folded neatly and placed downstage center (see fig. 1). Any *karaori* (brocade kimono) or *nuihaku* (kimono with needlework and gold—or silver—leaf imprint designs) with red in its design would serve. *Nuihaku* are often preferred because they are lighter, and the densely embroidered sixteenth-century *nuihaku* in The Art Institute of Chicago's collection (pl. 1; cat. no. 1) would be a most elegant choice. One of the Art Institute's *karaori* (see pl. 10; cat. no. 8) would add a further dimension—its design of interlocking circles and flower carts recalls an incident that festers in Rokujo's psyche. During a festival procession, the ox cart of Lady Aoi jostles that of Rokujo out of line, blocking her view and greatly embittering her. Circles, wheels, and the revolution of fate dominate the play's imagery.

Drawn by the twang of a shaman's catalpa bow, a beautiful woman (in fact, the wandering spirit of Rokujo) approaches the ailing body of Lady Aoi. The beautiful woman sidles up to the folded cloth, beats it, and retreats. Later, she returns as a snake figure with a horned mask and a scale pattern on her garments to batter the poor Aoi again, attacking her with a magic wand. Aoi, frail to begin with, has but a thread of identity left by the time Rokujo's wandering spirit is through with her and the priest has managed to quell her spirit with the help of incantations.[1]

In *Aoinoue*, the folded robe replaces a human being. In the play *Utō*, a part of a garment serves to identify a character. The ghost of a hunter waylays a wandering priest and requests that he ask his wife to set up a holy stupa—that is, a memorial reliquary mound—for his soul. Sure that word of mouth alone will be insufficient to convince her of his identity, he rips off his left sleeve and asks the priest to get her to verify it against his death robe. On reaching the house the priest presents the wife

with the ripped-off sleeve. Taking out his death robe woven with "crude wisteria bark," she finds one sleeve missing, and declares, "There can be no mistake. His thin, unlined summer robe matches the sleeve perfectly." Overcome with nostalgia, she asks the monk to pray for his soul.[2]

In the Nō play *Hagoromo* (*The Feather Robe*), the identity of a heavenly maiden of the moon is thematically linked to her feather robe. Without it, she tells Hakuryō, the fisherman who has found and picked up her garment while she was having a dip in the sea, she is unable to fly back to the sky and join her moon sisters. When the fisherman refuses to give back the robe, the signs of her celestial nature begin to fade, and even "the flowers in her hair wilt and droop."[3] The fisherman finally gives in, and, donning her feather robe (achieved by retreating to the rear of the stage and kneeling down so stage attendants can drape it over her shoulders, stitch it in place, and tie the strings in bows), she immediately regains her self-possession. In thanks, she performs the dances of "Rainbow Skirts" and "Feather Cloak."

The feather robe of the heavenly maiden completes her identity, and the sleeve of the hunter's robe in *Utō* acts as an identification card. In a similar way, the various elements of the dress of the *yamabushi*, the mountain ascetic or wandering monk, symbolize his religious powers. In the play *Ataka*, the warrior Minamoto Yoshitsune and his retainers are trying to escape persecution by traveling in the disguise of twelve *yamabushi*. Before reaching a barrier where they will be minutely scrutinized, the elegant Yoshitsune is urged to "exchange his brocaded robes for the crude hemp clothes" of the baggage carrier and to be sure to pull the broad hat of the carrier well over his face.[4] At the barrier, the sentinel demands their death. In *yamabushi* style, they say their last rites, enumerating the meaning of their costumes, according to a catechism still heard in *yamabushi* rites today:

The small round cap is a crown of the Five Wisdoms
The twelve pleats are the Twelve Causes.
The persimmon-colored brocaded cloth appears in the
  nine-fold *mandala*.
Black leggings for the black in the Womb *mandala*
And the eight-eyed straw sandals?
To tread on eight petaled lotus flowers.[5]

An amusing parody on this incantation of articles of clothing appears in the Kyōgen (or comic) play entitled *Kagyū*, or *The Snail*, which would be performed between the more serious Nō plays (see fig. 2). A man is told to procure some snails to present as a medicine for long life. Searching for something with "black on the head" and "shell on the hip" that sometimes "sticks out horns," the man comes upon a sleeping *yamabushi*. Sure enough, this must be a snail, he thinks, for it has black on the head (a small round cap, or *tokin*), a shell on the hip, (a conch shell the *yamabushi* blow to signal each other), and horns (the pompons decorating the vest). For a while the *yamabushi* leads the man on in his deception, and then the two go off the stage singing and dancing to a chant of "snail, snail, nail, nail, snail, snail, nail."[6]

In *Sotoba Komachi*, one finds a recitation of possessions reminiscent of the clothing incantation of the *yamabushi*. Over one hundred years old, the former beauty and poetess Ono no Komachi appears now as a destitute hag. While she once had "thin silk gauzes and patterned brocades innumerable," now all that is left of her identity are parched millet and beans in the pouch around her neck, and in the pouch on her back,

remnants,
her filthy garb, stained with dirt and oil. . .
Torn straw cloak
Torn bamboo hat. . .

"If only I had a sleeve," she wails, "to hold back my tears."[7]

Garments as Devices of Spirit Possession

As *Sotoba Komachi* continues, Komachi begins to beg with her bamboo hat (see fig. 3). The spirit within it takes hold of her, and the pent-up voice of a lover of long ago, Captain Fukakusa of the Fourth Rank, echoes through her body. His spirit describes how, in vain, he had gone

FIGURE 2. In this photograph of a contemporary performance of the Kyōgen (or comic) play *Kagyū*, the wandering *yamabushi* priest shows the conch shell on his hip to the gullible servant in order to convince him that he is indeed a snail carrying a shell on its back. Photo: Masakatsu Ushimado.

FIGURE 3. In this scene from a modern production of *Sotoba Komachi*, the aged Ono no Komachi begs with her straw hat. She wears a traveling cloak (*mizugoromo*), indicating her age as well as her miserable circumstances. Photo: Masakatsu Ushimado.

能樂百番
二人靜

up to her door for ninety-nine nights enduring rain and snow,

Hitching up his pure white trousers,
his lacquered courtier's cap wind-bent backward,
his hunting cloak's sleeve flipped over head.[8]

The visitation of the spirit of Captain Fukakusa in *Sotoba Komachi* comes like a sudden shower and departs abruptly.

The play *Futari Shizuka* presents the theme of possession in a more fully developed way. While gathering early spring herbs, a shrine girl is waylaid by a strange woman who demands that she go back to the shrine and ask the priests there to copy holy sutras (Buddhist precepts) for her, a form of prayer to ensure a soul safe passage after death. Returning to the shrine, the girl begins to give an evasive account of her adventure to the priests. But the impatient spirit of the mysterious woman invades the shrine girl and interrupts her narrative. To achieve this effect, the actor changes the quality of his voice, lowering the pitch and slowing his enunciation: "What do you mean? Incredible?"[9] Eventually, the spirit reveals that she once was Shizuka Gozen, the mistress of the valiant, yet hunted, Genji warrior Yoshitsune (see the description of the play *Ataka* above):

"Shizuka Gozen was a renown[ed] dancer, show us a step or two," demand the priests.
"My dancing costume was offered up to the deity of Katsute Shrine," she answers.
"What was the color of your dance costume?"
"The *hakama* skirts were of red silk."
"And the *suikan* robe?"
"[It is decorated with] myriad flowers from autumn fields."[10]

Donning the robe, which is indeed in the storage house, the shrine maiden begins to dance, trailing the flowing sleeves of the cloak, and behind her the real ghost of Shizuka looks on, seemingly manipulating her with invisible strings. Then Shizuka, too, enters the dance and two identical cloaks circle the stage side by side with gossamer sleeves swishing in complete unison (see fig. 4). A single being has produced a double image through the transference of a garment.[11]

Time, too, has doubled up as memories accumulate. Both women chant together:

Shizu ya shizu	Whirring, whirring
shizu ya odamaki	bobbins of humble women
kurikaeshi	turning, turning
mukashi o ima ni.	the past into now.[12]

(The sound of *shizu* begins the name *Shizuka* and means both "quiet, still" and "lower-class woman.")

The type of possessed dance presented in *Futari Shizuka* is known as an *utsurimai*, a dance performed by

FIGURE 5. In the Nō play *Izutsu*, the wife of Ariwara no Narihira dresses in her late husband's court cap and robe. As she peers into the well (represented figuratively onstage) that was the setting for their childhood romance, she sees his reflection in her own. Although the hat she wears is indeed a court cap, her *chōken* bears little resemblance to a Heian courtier's cloak; this, however, presents no hindrance to the imagination of the Nō audience, for the *chōken* is a standard costume for a female role with a long dance in the second half of a play. Photo: Masakatsu Ushimado.

FIGURE 4. Tsukioka Kogyo. *Futari Shizuka*, early twentieth century. Print no. 27 from the series *Nōgaku hyakuban* (vol. 2). Woodblock print; 25.9 x 38 cm. The Art Institute of Chicago, Bequest of Henry C. Schwab Estate (1943.834). The theme of doubling in *Futari Shizuka* is dramatized when a shrine maiden and the ghost of Shizuka Gozen, the mistress of a Genji warrior, dance in unison in identical costumes.

the spirit of another that has entered the body, generally through the donning of a robe. It has its origins in ancient Shinto rituals, where the shrine maiden, *miko*, functioned also as a shaman. Possessed dances can be found as well in Korean shamanistic practices. *Utsurimai* appear in quite a number of Nō plays, particularly plays about women.

In the play *Matsukaze*, two sisters who live on Suma beach collecting brine to make into salt cannot free themselves from their attachment, even after his death, to their one-time lover, the poet and courtier Ariwara no Yukihira. In particular, the older sister, Pine Wind (Matsukaze), recalling the parting poem of Yukihira in which he promises to return "if she pines for him" (a deliberate pun), becomes quite deranged. The cloak and hat that Yukihira left behind seem to her to be the man himself. Donning the garments (a *monogi*, or onstage costume change), she now mistakes a pine tree (a stage prop and a memorial to the girls as well as a central symbol in the play) for Yukihira. Her more realistic sister tries to dissuade her of the illusion, but Pine Wind only enters deeper into madness and rushes to embrace the pine tree "Yukihira." The sleeves of his former robe envelope the symbol of his memory.[13]

In *Matsukaze*, the donning of the robe of a former lover has precipitated a mad scene where time is collapsed and wishes become reality. More commonly the donning of the robe creates a double identity. In *Izutsu*, for example, the devoted and constant wife of the playboy Ariwara no Narihira (Yukihira's brother, and a subject of the tenth-century poetic sketches *Tales of Ise*) dons her late husband's robe and momentarily becomes one with him:

In his clothes I appear
as the Man of Long Ago.
Court cap and gown—
then, no longer a woman:
a man, I have become
Narihira's image.[14]

She looks down into the well that inspired their childhood romance, and the double image of man in woman fills her with nostalgia (see fig. 5).

The doubling of identities that occurs in *Izutsu* with the putting on of a robe becomes more complex in the Nō play *Kakitsubata* (*The Iris*). A monk on his way to the eastern lands comes to a swamp filled with blooming irises and traversed by a web of eight bridges. When a young lady appears, he gets her to recite a poem composed in that very spot by the same poet-lover Ariwara no Narihira when he was exiled from the capital because of an illicit relationship:

Karakoromo	China robe
kitsutsu narenishi	worn through with love
tsuma shi areba	by my absent wife:
harubaru kinuru	far, far, I have come
tabi o shi zo omou.	traveling with heavy heart.[15]

This is an acrostic, with the first syllable of each line spelling *kakitsubata* (*ha* can be read *ba*), or iris. It also uses clothing imagery to express Narihira's deep longing for the woman he has left behind. As can be seen below, the opening *karakoromo* is a standard epithet (*makura-kotoba*, or pillow word) for "to wear" (*kiru*), which in certain conjugations sounds identical with "to come." A similar wordplay runs through the whole poem, with

FIGURE 6. In the Kyōgen play *Futari Daimyo*, a passerby is asked by two *daimyo* (or samurai) lords to carry their swords. The passerby, however, uses the swords to force the *daimyo* to strip down to their leggings and perform silly dances. Photo: Kawanabe Gyōsai (painter), *Sketches of Nō* (1887).

clothing-related words forming a minor theme (underlining indicates words associated with clothing):

karakoromo
China <u>robe</u> (elegant, like the karaori)

kitsutsu	*narenishi*
<u>worn</u> and <u>worn</u>	till soft
come	having grown fond of

tsuma shi areba
wife I have, so
<u>robe hem</u>

harubaru	*kinuru*
distant	I have come
<u>stretch cloth</u>	<u>wear</u>

tabi o shi zo omou
traveling: (sad) thoughts

Later the young maid dons a *chōken*, or cloak, that is purple like an iris, as well as a cap and a sword, thereby taking on the being of the poet-lover Narihira himself (see pl. 14; cat. no. 11).[16] She calls to the monk, "Look here, a court cap and Chinese robe." He exclaims that she is "wearing a robe of radiant color and a young man's court cap. What can it mean?" She replies, "This is that very Chinese robe sung of in the poem, the *karakoromo* worn by Empress Takako. The court cap, Narihira wore when he performed the ceremonial dance of *gosechi* in autumn."

Next she discloses that she is in fact the spirit of the iris, about whom the poem was composed. As the threads of imagery in the play interweave, she becomes as well the memory of Narihira's love. And since he was the god of Music and Dance incarnate, she dances in celebration of his divinity. The robe and hat accumulate meanings of their own. The sleeves of the dancing robe "turn back" (*sode o kaesu*, a standard phrase evoking the fluttering of broad sleeves when a person dances) to the capital, and the lining bears traces of bitterness (*ura* means lining, *urameshi* means bitter feeling). The hat worn as a "cap of manhood" is also known as the "coming-of-age hat."

The play ends in a swirl of images interrelated by the incantation of numerous names for types of irises and the evocation of the color purple. Like the "cicada which casts off its empty Chinese robe for sleeves of dazzling white," the heart of the iris unfurls to enlightenment. The monk awakens to the purpling sky from a dream of paradise.

The Art Institute's collection includes a *nuihaku* that features a navy blue and silver checkerboard ground as well as embroidered patterns of irises with bridges illustrates the scene in the *Tales of Ise* on which *Kakitsubata* is based (see pl. 4; cat. no. 2). Various colored irises rise out of water represented by swerving lines etched in silver.

Swaying irises border the edges of overlapping rectangular planks. The theme, rendered here against background colors reminiscent of the night sky with a luminescent moon (symbol of the enlightenment that the spirit of the iris seeks), is a favorite not only for *nuihaku*, but also for fan decorations and standing screens. The most famous are those of the eighteenth-century artist Ogata Kōrin that can be seen in the Nezu Art Museum, Tokyo.

A Nō actor performing *Kakitsubata* might well choose a *nuihaku* with iris motifs to wear in the second part of the play. It would be wrapped snugly around the legs and tied at the waist; the upper half would be folded down with the sleeves hanging over the hips (*koshimaki* style). A white *surihaku* in satin weave would be worn under it, but this would be barely visible on the upper half of the body when covered by Narihira's robe, a purple *chōken*. (For an example of a *surihaku* in the Art Institute's collection, see pl. 6, cat. no. 4.)

Garments as Gifts

Since prehistoric times, cloth has played a central role in the economics of Japanese society and in maintaining personal relationships. In 243, the Japanese princess Himiko is said to have returned a gift of silk from China with natively woven silks and colored cloths. Beginning in the Nara period (710–794) and continuing until the nineteenth century, textile-related products (silk thread, cloth, clothing, dyes) were a major item of tribute and of tax payment. Records verify that, by the fourteenth century, Nō actors received a portion of their wages in cloth. Bonus payment came in the form of appreciative members of the audience stripping their cloaks and throwing them on stage.[17]

The custom of stripping is presented comically in the Kyōgen play *Futari Daimyo*. Here two *daimyo* look for someone to carry their swords. The man they find uses the weapons he is forced to carry to threaten the pretentious lords and get them to strip off layers of clothing down to their underwear (fig. 6). After he has forced them to perform a number of debasing roles, he runs off with the clothes and swords as well.

Only slightly less monetary in purpose is the Japanese custom of giving garments on special occasions. In the tenth-century novel *The Tale of Genji*, the hero Hikaru Genji goes to considerable lengths to choose the right robes to give to each of his girlfriends for the New Year's celebration. He must match colors with their station and sensibility.

Naturally, the topic of gifts of textiles appears in Nō plays, as well. In the play *Miwa*, a woman gives a secluded monk, Genpin Sōzu, a present of fresh water every day. It is a small gift that effectively piques his curiosity to ask her who she is. Although her answer to his question is

能樂
百番

三輪

evasive, she has a request of her own: will he lend her a robe, for the nights are getting cold? She leaves with the garment, but later in the play Genpin is brought by a villager to the shrine of the god of Miwa, where he finds his robe hanging between two cedar trees with a poem attached:

Three circles
clean and clear:
The Chinese cloak,
not to be thought of as given
nor as taken.[18]

In this very intricate poem, which can be read on many levels in the original Japanese, we have the essence of true giving—no strings attached, a flow from soul to soul. The giving in the play has only begun, for soon the god appears from behind the symbolic robe, a woman in male attire.

Seen in the form of a woman
the deity of Miwa
dressed not in the garb of a priestess
but attired as a priest
with lacquer hat and hunting cloak
draped over skirts.

The doubling of sexes appears here in a different context from the union of lover and loved. The sex of the god of Miwa is an enigma. Clearly the mysterious character who gives water to the monk is female, and, if one believes the statement at the end of the play that "the deity of Miwa and the Sun Goddess are one and the same," then the deity must be a she. But according to the story related in the narrative *kuse* section of the play, the deity of Miwa is definitely male.

This tale is a Japanese rendition of the story of Cupid and Psyche. It relates how a young wife is induced by her parents to ask her husband why he comes to her only at night. He answers that he is too ashamed to show his true form, and that this must be their last meeting. She quickly picks up her needle and stitches into his garment, leaving a long thread to trail behind him. Following the thread, she is led to the base of the two cedars that mark the shrine of the deity of Miwa. There she finds the end of the thread coiled into three circles (*mi-wa*): the three rings of the gift, the giver, and the receiver; or the *sanrin* (written with the same characters), the three agents of human action: the body, the mouth, and the spirit.

On hearing this story, the monk Genpin rejoices in the gift he has been given and asks for more. The deity next relates in dance the story of the Sun Goddess being trapped in a cave and lured out by a dance performance (see fig. 7). Just as in *Hagoromo*, where the feather robe was exchanged for a heavenly dance to be treasured by

FIGURE 7. Tsukioka Kogyo. *Miwa*, early twentieth century. Print no. 44 from the series *Nōgaku hyakuban* (vol. 1). Woodblock print; 25.9 x 38 cm. The Art Institute of Chicago, Bequest of Henry C. Schwab Estate (1943.833). In this scene, the deity of Miwa performs a Shinto dance (*kagura*) for the monk Genpin in return for his gift of a robe.

FIGURE 8. As portrayed in this woodblock print from the collection of the Nishijin-ori Kaikan, Kyoto, the traditional Japanese draw loom (*sorabiki-bata*) required a team of workers to create textiles made of silk. The ground weave was manipulated by foot pedals while the pattern warps were picked up in a set order at appropriate moments by the draw boy sitting atop the loom. Photo: Alan Kennedy, *Japanese Costume: History and Tradition* (Paris, 1990), p. 30.

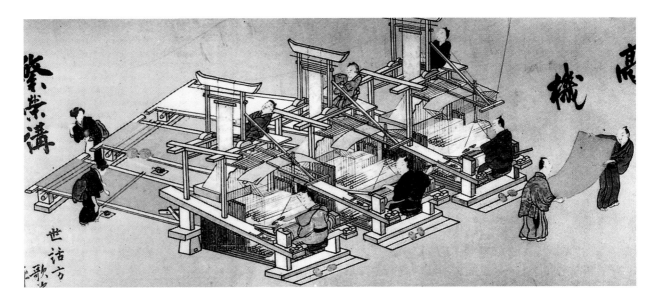

FIGURE 9. The making of textiles has a symbolic role in the Nō play *Adachigahara*. As the old woman winds thread onto a large bobbin, she complains to the audience that it is the "long and painful" thread of life. Her mesh traveling cloak (*yore mizugoromo*) is produced by pulling the loose weave out of shape after it is off the loom. Photo: Monica Bethe.

mankind, so here, too, a heavenly dance is presented in return for a robe.

Sewing, Weaving, and Spinning

In *Miwa*, the young wife takes up her needle and thread and symbolically stitches into a garment. In other Nō plays, images of textile production appear as leitmotifs. Typical of these leitmotifs is the figurative cloth *tsukushi*, or listing of images associated with cloth. We noted one such listing above in the acrostic on "*kakitsubata*." Of the plays mentioned so far, listings of textile-related images appear also in *Matsukaze*, *Aoinoue*, *Izutsu*, *Utō*, and *Sotoba Komachi*. Words that typically appear in such listings include types and parts of clothing (particularly sleeves, hems, linings, and the overlap of the kimono), actions related to dressing (such as putting on, taking off, and tying clothes), and actions related to textile production and care (such as spinning, weaving, sewing, winding bobbins, stretching cloth to remove creases, and fulling to soften cloth).

The play *Kureha* reads like one long weaving *tsukushi*. The play alludes to a passage in the eighth-century *Chronicles of Japan* (*nihon shokki*, book 10) in which Achi no Omi brought four women skilled in the textile arts back from the Chinese country of Wu (read Kure in Japanese) as presents for Emperor Ōjin (270–310). These women, later deified, passed on the secrets of their art and became the ancestors of Japanese weavers of pat-

terned cloths, like the many-colored *nishiki* and the figured twill (*aya*), and, by extension, also the brocaded silks used for Nō costumes like the *karaori* and *atsuita*.

This Nō play is set in the town of Kureha, or "Wu Weaving." The central characters are two weaving girls named Kurehatori and Ayahatori. Kurehatori is "one who weaves on a Wu loom" while Ayahatori is "one who weaves on an *aya* loom." Together they produce an array of cloths. Kurehatori sits at the loom; Ayahatori "picks up and pulls the threads." This has been interpreted by some as meaning she spins, or winds bobbins. Considering, however, that the women are producing a complex patterned cloth, she may be pulling the heddle strings on a draw loom (see fig. 8). The sounds of the shuttle flying and the beater pounding reverberate, culminating in a final dance passage where the clatter of repeated "ta" sounds (*tanabata no tamatama aeru tabitito . . .*) expands the scene up to heaven where the Sky Weaving Girl (*tanabata*, or the star Vega) joins in producing "treasured figured cloth" (*takara no aya o oritate oritate*). With a swish of the fan, the dancer honors the loom and bestows its elegant produce on the emperor. In some performances, the imagery is further enhanced by placing on midstage a large loom prop strung with colorful ribbons.[19]

The first step in setting up a loom in preparation for weaving is to wind the threads onto bobbins. The play *Adachigahara*, also known as *Kurozuka*, presents a bobbin-winding scene in which an old woman takes up a hand wheel and slowly rotates it; the eyes of the wooden mask eerily follow the thread as it winds on the bobbins (see fig. 9). The thread she winds becomes the thread of life—"long and painful," she complains. In fact, this is but a disguise to cut the life thread of her unexpected visitors, for later she reveals her true form: a man-eating ogress.[20]

After the cloth is woven, it must be softened and made glossy. For this procedure, two women sit on opposite sides of a cloth-padded board, known as a fulling block, and alternately pound cloth laid over the board. The play *Kinuta (The Fulling Block)* centers on a woman who pounds desperately on the fulling block, a small prop placed in center stage, in the hope that the sound of her beating will reverberate across many miles of land and sea to reach her husband, who is delayed in the capital. In the passage below, I have abbreviated a long scene that begins and ends with mimed beating on the block:

the block of angry pain
beat it; beat
the robe, cold
whistling wind
send the message . . .
Not too violently . . .
do not rip his dreams:
once dreams are broken
who will wear this robe?
If he returns, forever,
the robe shall be refashioned.
Still, summer clothes make thin promises . . .
(She begins to beat the block again)
A thousand ten thousand voices
of grief
if only their message reaches him. . . .
The pounding on the fulling block,
the wailing of night gales,
the shrill voices of insects
mix with the sobs of dripping dew
horohoro harhara harato.
Which is the sound of the fulling block?[21]

She dies in the effort, but when her husband returns and prays for her soul, the wrathful beating that occasioned her death becomes the tool for her salvation.

Dressing for the Occasion

The elaborate rules of etiquette that pervade Japanese life make appropriate dress extremely important. Choosing just the right colors to match the season, occasion, and one's status is an art much revered and carefully taught. In Nō drama, we see this conscious calculation of attire both in the rules set down by a tradition that specifies a particular combination of layers of garments for each role, and in passages of text describing attire. Examples of

the latter have been quoted above in references to *Miwa* and *Kakitsubata.*

Another example appears in the play *Kayoi Komachi.* Komachi's suitor, Captain Fukakusa (see *Sotoba Komachi* above), must come to Komachi's doorstep for one hundred nights before she will give in to him. Each night, this nobleman disguised in a bamboo hat and straw cape, steals across town to mark a notch in the shaft of her carriage. Finally, the hundredth night comes. In high anticipation of at last being let into her dwelling, he exchanges his rags for finery. No actual costume change breaks the flow of action, but the words are underscored with dramatic gestures:

Wretched bamboo hat	(he looks at hat in right hand)
I replace with an elegant court cap.	(tosses hat away)
The straw cape I shed	(mimes slipping off cloak by circling right hand up and out to the side)
for flower-patterned robe	(displays sleeves, holding out first the left, then the right in *sayu* pattern)
of layered hues.	(completes the presentation)
Light purple are my	(stepping back, spreads arms)
wisteria-colored pantaloons	(focuses attention on the pants by placing the tips of the fingers of the left hand on the left leg and looking at it)[22]

In most plays, however, costume change is integral to the unfolding of the plot. We have seen instances of the donning of a robe on the main stage in full view of the audience (*monogi*) in *Matsukaze, Kakitsubata, Futari Shizuka,* and *Hagoromo.* More often costume changes are done between acts, during the action, in the dressing room backstage, or inside a covered prop placed at the rear of the stage. A figure who seems to be of this world—a young woman, say, or an old man—reappears as a ghost, demon, or god. Stripped of the guise of normal time and space, lured by the hum of sutras being chanted, the figure returns in the wee hours of the morning, its true form revealed. Thus runs the basic plot of "dream" Nō plays (*mugen nō*).

The typical costume change involves taking off a layer or two of garments and replacing them, in most cases, with more voluminous robes and cloaks draped and stitched in place in a manner appropriate for the type of movement to be performed (in most instances, the second half of a play centers around a dance). In *Yamamba,* for example, an old woman waylays the dancer Hyakuma Yamamba on a pilgrimage through the mountains. She wears the tightly wrapped, sober-colored *karaori* that inhibits the size of her steps. After questioning Hyakuma Yamamba about the true nature of the real Yamamba whom Hyakuma presumes to impersonate in her dances,

the old woman declares she will reveal the real identity of Yamamba and then vanishes. She reappears "in form and speech human, yet," like a demon, she has "snow-covered brambles for hair, eyes shining like stars, and cheeks the color of vermilion."²³ She wears a voluminous costume suited to energetic action (see fig. 10). The choice of garments contains an enigma: the geometrically patterned *atsuita* (a brocaded garment of the same shape as the *karaori* with a more dynamic design), which is worn as an undergarment by demons, is draped here as an outer cloak in the style a court woman would wear a *karaori* (*tsuboori*). Her divided skirts are not the plain-colored *ōguchi* worn by women, but the boldly brocaded *hangiri* worn by supernatural beings (see pl. 17; cat. no. 15).

Despite her fearful appearance, Yamamba pleads to be recognized for her deeds of kindness. Realizing this desire lies at the root of delusion, she "casts it all away, and dragging good and evil, makes her mountain rounds." Round and round she circles the stage, pinned to the wheel of Buddhist law, and as "dust piles up to become a mountain, so she becomes...a mountain-crone." In a variant performance called *Shirogashira*, each word of this line of text is enacted with costume manipulation:

dust piles up	the actor unties his *atsuita* and, crouching, draws it over his head to encase his body
mountain	he begins to rise, covered by the robe
crone	while standing, he lifts both arms, displaying the form of Yamamba backed by the dark lining of the *atsuita*
becomes	he drops the garment and moves off at lightning speed, leaping over peaks and peering into valleys.²⁴

The consummation of Yamamba's identity, central to her quest for enlightenment, finds its final form in stripping away layers of clothing, just as earlier she had cast off delusions through enacting her own tale. In shedding her clothing, Yamamba sheds misinterpretations in an opposite process from the women in *Izutsu*, *Matsukaze*, and *Kakitsubata*, who, in donning extra layers of clothing, assume other identities.

The visual impact of Nō costumes as they identify the sex, status, and profession of individual characters, and as they are used in performance, supports and reflects the poetic text of the Nō play, itself ornamented with textile imagery. This type of give-and-take between the elements of a performance lies at the core of the Nō aesthetic. The whole is far more than a sum of its parts, yet each of the parts is a whole in itself. The costume as a work of art, separated from the stage and its props, from the actor's gestures, and from the poetry and music of a performance, nonetheless contains the same process of give-and-take. In a brocaded robe like the *karaori* or *atsuita*, the variation of color in each visual motif creates an ever-changing overall image despite the mechanically fixed repeated pattern. The eyes wander from sleeve to hem to body of the robe, focusing for a moment on an exquisite detail, then refocusing to enjoy the interplay of shapes, until the motifs and colors expand to create a complete vision.

FIGURE 10. The enigma of the identity of the Old Woman of the Mountains (Yamamba) can be seen in her costume: the pants (*hangiri*) and brocaded *atsuita*, which are both male garments, are draped in a style reserved for a female robe (*karaori*). The *karaori* is customarily used to represent women of the court, women suffering in hell, and sprites. Photo: Masakatsu Ushimado.

Nō Drama Costumes and Other Japanese Costumes in The Art Institute of Chicago

MARY V. HAYS and RALPH E. HAYS

Los Gatos, California

The Japanese costumes in the permanent collection of The Art Institute of Chicago that are presented here range from a sixteenth-century Momoyama period *nuihaku*, a rare early Nō costume, to an informal outer coat, *haori*, of the twentieth century. As a group, these costumes comprise one of the finer collections of Japanese garments outside Japan.

Each of these costumes will be described following an introduction that is in two parts. First, the aesthetics of Japanese costume is discussed in relation to the origins of the motifs seen in textile patterning and the symbolism inherent in these designs. This is followed by a brief summary of the development of the Nō theater with an emphasis on the importance of the costume in the creation of a role.

Symbolism and the Japanese Aesthetic

Dramatic expression is an integral part of the patterning of Japanese costume. The motifs in the patterning and the colors used create not only a beautiful design or picture but often silently in their symbolism they convey hidden meanings. They may refer to a well-known legend, literary work, or folk tales. The symbols used may create a mood, evoke a season, or express an ideal. Humor is sometimes present in sly allusions to recognizable objects or events. Since the Japanese language is rich in homophonic sounds, the pronunciation of a word or character while sounding the same can have more than one meaning. Therefore, motifs may be puns.

The wordless expression of latent emotions or intellectual concepts is rooted in the animism of the ancient beliefs of an agricultural society. After the advent of Buddhism in Japan, in A.D. 538, in order to distinguish the native beliefs from Buddhist doctrine, these earlier beliefs and rituals were called Shinto, the "Way of the Gods," with worship centered on the gods who dwelt in mountains, hills, and rocks; valleys, plains, and rice paddies; in water in the form of rain, mist, clouds, lakes, rivers, and waterfalls; and in the seemingly supernatural forces of wind and fire. By the early fifth century, Chinese cultural influences, such as the practical ethics of Confucianism, the Taoist dualism of the Yin and Yang, and the Five Elements of Wood, Earth, Fire, Metal, and Water had begun to affect the social customs and the legends of the Japanese.[1]

During the Nara period (710–794), the ancient legends of the gods responsible for the genesis of Japan were compiled in the *Kojiki* (*The Record of Ancient Matters*) and in the *Nihon Shoki* (*The Beginning of Japan*), also called the *Nihongi*. The purpose of these chronicles was partly to legitimate the lineage of the Japanese sovereigns, and in so doing they emulated the Chinese dynastic historians.[2] In time, certain creatures—animals, birds, and insects—became associated with the gods of these

FIGURE 1. *Furisode* (detail of pl. 24), Late Edo period, nineteenth century. Silk, 4/1 satin damask weave, *rinzu*; yuzen dyed, painted, stenciled, and embroidered with silk and gold-leaf-paper-strip-wrapped cotton in satin and single-satin stitches; laid work, couching, and Chinese knots; lined with red silk, plain weave; dyed with *beni*, safflower; 183.7 x 122.7 cm. The Art Institute of Chicago, Gift of Gaylord Donnelley in memory of Frances Gaylord Smith (1991.635). See cat. no. 21. For more information on this costume and all other Art Institute costumes reproduced in this issue, see the comprehensive catalogue on pp. 37–40.

legends, and also numerous inanimate objects denoting their power were given anthropomorphic attributes. Such motifs became a part of the traditional vocabulary of Japanese design. Akihiko Takemura wrote, "Since there are no images for the Japanese gods of Shinto origin, their individuality has been expressed indirectly through the motifs used to identify them."[3] Many of these motifs are associated with Nō dramas that are based on Shinto legends and as symbols have become a part of the patterning of Nō costumes. They are motifs also used in the patterning of the formal *kosode* worn by the people.

The Chinese influence on Japanese design during the Asuka period (552–710) has been succinctly described by Ken Kirihata, Researcher of Weaving and Dyeing, Kyoto National Museum:

In Japan *karayo* (Chinese style) was the dominant style of beauty until the Nara period, 710–793. For example, in the designs of the flowering plants, *hōsoge* and *karahana*, are flowers no one has ever seen. They are imaginary flowers that bloom in mountains inhabited by immortals, the Pure Land of Buddhism or in the Persian paradise. The people living in the world dominated by *karayo* loved these flowers as symbols of eternal life.[4]

Although by the Heian period (794–1192) the life of the court society and the intellectuals was firmly grounded in Buddhist doctrine and the principles of Confucianism, the leisure and prosperity provided by a period of prolonged peace permitted the development of a distinctly Japanese aesthetic. There was a turning away from artistic inspiration derived from things unseen or not native to Japan and a reawakening of the innate Japanese sensibility to the beauty of their own natural surroundings and the animism that had been retained from their early beliefs. Mr. Kirihata points out that by the middle of the Heian period the preference of the courtiers was for this Japanese style of beauty, *wayō*. He illustrates this by a quotation from "The Broom-like Tree" chapter of Lady Murasaki's Heian novel, *The Tale of Genji*,[5] in which the effect on the viewer of the two styles of painting popular in that period are contrasted. The Chinese style that uses vivid, fanciful images of unknown or unreal subjects is startling to the viewer because they are "neither real nor true." Ordinary scenery sketched "almost to rival Nature. . .carries the spectator in imagination to something beyond them." This is the Japanese style of beauty to be found in familiar things realistically drawn and easily recognizable. It is preferred because these universally recognizable objects of Japanese origin express something beyond their explicit delineation that can deeply stir the innermost psyche. This preference underlines the romantic nature of the Japanese people who throughout history, even in the modern industrial age, continue to delight and find

meaning in the natural beauty of their homeland. The common people have always embraced the beliefs of Shintoism and the romantic symbolism of beautiful things, whether of nature or created by man, which has its roots in the original Shinto beliefs in the anthropomorphic powers assigned to natural phenomena. The patterning of the Nō costumes and the other *kosode* in the current exhibition, most of which date from the Edo period (1603–1868), is based on a distinctly Japanese idea of beauty and the drama that may be hidden in the composition of the design.

Objects that recall various aspects of Heian culture and scenes illustrating episodes of the literature of the period, especially *The Tale of Genji*, were used frequently in the Edo period for the patterning of *kosode*. The influence of Chinese Confucianism, however, was dominant once again in this period because the Tokugawa shogunate considered Confucian ethics necessary as a justification for their totalitarian regime. Consequently, the literati of the late Edo period were well versed in the culture of China, especially the Confucian Twenty-Four Tales of Filial Piety. Objects associated with these and other Chinese legends appear in *kosode* patterning. The dragon, the phoenix, and other supernatural animals, as well as imaginary floral forms, all introduced when Chinese culture first influenced Japanese design, also

Japanese Historical Periods

TUMULUS		c. 250 – 552
ASUKA		552 – 710
NARA		710 – 794
HEIAN		794 – 1192
KAMAKURA		1192 – 1336
MUROMACHI		1336 – 1568
MOMOYAMA		1568 – 1603
EDO		1603 – 1868
	EARLY	1603 – 1716
	MIDDLE	1716 – 1789
	LATE	1789 – 1868
MEIJI		1868 – 1912
TAISHO		1912 – 1926
SHOWA		1926 – 1989
HEISEI		1989 –

were used. Even these motifs were subtly transformed to comply with the Japanese style of natural beauty preferred for *kosode* patterning.

Nō Drama and Its Development as Related to Costume

In order to appreciate how the twenty or so types of Nō costumes are used for various roles and why their color or patterning may determine the choice of costume, it is necessary to understand both the nature of Nō drama and how it developed.

Nō is a highly stylized music drama in which the revelation of the truth and beauty of the story is achieved through the constant building-up of a single emotional experience or the creation of the atmospheric conditions essential to the dramatic action. Although the music and the plot are the framework of the action, the dramatic experience shared by the audience is brought to a climax by the principal actor, the *shite*, through the many movements of the dance. Donald Keene, who has written extensively on the Nō drama, analyzed the relationship between the slow-moving poetic quality of Nō, the long periods in which there may be no action whatsoever, and the dances involving extraordinary movement:

The Nō repertory comprises a great variety of works, ranging from virtually static celebrations of the glories of a particular shrine to pieces of violent movement in which devils assert their terrible powers. It includes works which are almost purely poetic and symbolic, suggesting the loveliness of plum blossoms or the snow, and others of betrayal and vengeance . . . the slow-moving poetic works give Nō its meaning and ultimate appeal.[6]

Keene points out the significance of the actor's movements in the dance: "The final dance is extremely important in Nō, and may make reading the plays seem only a shell of the whole work, but the dance itself is not so much a display of agility or brilliance of movement as a continuation in a different idiom of the mood created by the motionlessness."[7] To achieve this very purpose, the masks and costumes worn have been refined in every detail of color, pattern, and style to conform with the manner in which these moods will be expressed. They are major works of art from which the actor makes his choice after deciding how he will interpret the role.

The many types of costumes worn today gradually developed over the centuries as Nō changed from a shrine ritual to the ceremonial entertainment of the Tokugawa shogunate. Nō originally meant "a performance." The Chinese character for Nō means "to be able," which can be interpreted to mean "possessing an ability" and, as applied to a drama, "possessing the ability to perform."[8] Until the latter half of the fourteenth century, Nō drama consisted of plays performed as rituals at shrines. These plays were called *Sarugaku no Nō*, "Monkey-music per-

formance." Originally this strange name was used to facetiously describe the licentious buffoonery that was performed as an antidote to the solemnity of the Shinto song-dance called *Kagura*. Before the middle of the fourteenth century, however, *Sarugaku no Nō* had become a serious dramatic performance and was a rival of *Dengaku no Nō*, a "Field-music performance," another serious musical drama that had originated in the rustic exhibitions of acrobatics and juggling. Eventually, *Sarugaku no Nō* became a "new kind of performance, including elements of the *Dengaku*; the *Kōwaku*, a recitation, accompanied by rhythmical tapping with the fan; the *Kuse-mai* or chanted-dance . . .; the *Kōuta* or danced popular-ballad . . .; and the *Bugaku* or Chinese Court dance."[9] The actors were inner members of the shrine and the purpose of the plays was to recite the legends of the shrine; to pray for peace, a bountiful harvest, and continued prosperity for future generations; purification by vanquishing evil spirits; and to tell folk legends and stories of a mother's sufferings at the loss of a child.

In the early part of the Muromachi period (1336–1568), the third Ashikaga shogun, Yoshimitsu (1358–1408), and the upper echelon of the military class became interested in the *Sarugaku no Nō*, and became patrons of the finest actors. Under the influence of the actors Kan'ami (1333–1384) and his son Zeami (1363–1443?), *Sarugaku no Nō* was developed into the drama known today as Nō.

The military aristocracy of the Muromachi period felt inferior to the old court aristocracy rooted in the culture of the Heian period. By using such Heian court literature as the *Tales of Ise* and *The Tale of Genji* as inspiration for his Nō dramas, Zeami attempted to immerse the military class in the culture of the Heian period. Of course, the actors who played the roles of Heian court officials needed luxurious garments. Ken Kirihata wrote that, when a Nō performance

was especially well received, the shogun and feudal lords present would rise, strip off their own garments and donate them on the spot. According to the *Tadasu-gawara Kanju Sarugaku Nikki* (records of the *sarugaku* performances on the riverbank near Tadasu) of 1463, in three days no fewer than 273 garments were donated in this fashion.[10]

In time, these "strippings" were designated according to the kind of garment removed. The act was referred to as "stripping *kosode*," "stripping *suō*," and so on.[11]

Nō costumes worn for aristocratic roles in the medieval period did not differ from the garments worn everyday by the members of the upper classes. After the third Tokugawa shogun, Iemitsu (r. 1623–1651), Nō costumes "began to have certain characteristics different from the everyday wear which previously had made up part of [the] wardrobe of the actors. They came to be produced specifically for the stage and within the context of the high art of noh."[12] This change came about because Nō drama changed from simply an entertainment to a solemn ceremonial art performed for the ruling military class.

Over the years, the names given to the various categories of Nō plays have varied. Today the plays usually are divided into five groups:

(1) God plays, *kaminō*; also called *waki Nō*.
(2) Warrior-courtier plays called *shuranō*, after the battlefield in hell where the ghost warriors replay their battles. They are also called *shura mono*.
(3) Plays about women, named after the wig, *katsura*, worn for female roles. They are called *kazuranō*, using a different spelling of *katsura*, and also *katsura mono*.
(4) Some sources call this group *zatsu nō*, miscellaneous plays. They are also known as *genzaimono*, the contemporary category. Since many of the plays in this miscellany concern deranged women, they are known also as *kyōjo mono*, the crazed women category, or *monogurui*, which means literally "mad women" plays.
(5) Plays concerning demons are called *kichiku mono* and are performed at the end of a program. They are known also as final plays, *kirinō*.

A contemporary performance usually consists of three Nō plays, each play from a different group, performed in a prescribed order. In addition, there is one comic interlude of a Kyōgen play. There are five schools of Nō: Kanze, Hōshō, Kita, Komparu, and Kongō. "Each has slight differences in atmosphere, acting style, libretti, and use of masks and costumes."[13]

The Significance of the Actor's Choice of Mask and Costume

A Nō drama requires very few performers and the stage has no scenery except a painting of the ancient Yōgo Pine (at the Kasuga Shrine in Nara) on the wall behind the main stage. Donald Keene wrote of the importance of the costume under these austere circumstances:

The brilliance of the Nō costumes relieves the performances from any impression of excessive severity that might be created by the astringent bareness of the stage, the harsh cries of the musicians, and the formal gestures of the dancers.[14]

Because the costume and the mask are so important, "A Nō actor often spends days contemplating the mask he plans to use for a single performance, choosing and re-choosing the costume he will wear with it. The final ensemble is similar to a painting or a musical composition."[15] The minute an actor appears on the stage, a person in the audience versed in the Nō drama can tell from the mask and the costume chosen by the performer and the manner in which it is worn exactly how the actor will interpret the role.

In her essay "Color in Noh Costumes," Monica Bethe describes the importance of the colors of the costumes:

On the bare, unadorned noh stage, the costumes stand out for their resplendent colors. The rich hues of the garments. . .fill the stage, evoking an atmosphere of spring or fall and mirroring the hearts of the characters portrayed. Colors indicate rank, age and occupation. Colors also carry symbolic impact within the context of a play.[16]

For example, *karaori* costumes with red in the ground weave worn by an actor playing the role of a young woman are designated as *iro iri*, meaning "with color," but those worn for the role of an older woman are described as *iro nashi*, meaning "without color," which indicates that red is not used in the ground weave (although there may be some red in the patterning).

Nō Costumes in The Art Institute of Chicago Collection

Most of the Nō costumes in the Art Institute's collection are of the late Edo period, but one outstanding costume is a sixteenth-century *nuihaku* from the early part of the Momoyama period (pls. 1–3; cat. no. 1). According to Iwao Nagasaki, Curator of Textiles in the Department of Applied Arts at the Tokyo National Museum, "This is the only example of a Momoyama Period Noh costume in overseas collections. . . .The design and quality indicate that it is equivalent in value to the one in the Tokyo National Museum."[17]

The styling of this *nuihaku* is typical of the *kosode* of the Momoyama period with its wide body, close-fitting collar, long neck band, and the original width of the sleeves, which were very narrow. At a later date, pieces of another Momoyama *nuihaku* were added to the sleeves to widen them so that they would conform to the style of a later period Nō costume (see pl. 2). Thus the Art Institute is fortunate to have not only an entire garment made of the sixteenth-century fabric called *nuihaku* but also large fragments from another *nuihaku* garment of the same period.

The all-over patterning of this *nuihaku* is unusual in its variety of motifs. The large, tiered lozenges reminiscent of pine bark, called *matsu kawa bishi*, are red on the left side of the garment and filled with embroidered willow branches laden with snow. In contrast, the lozenges on the right side are white and filled with a variety of embroidered plants and flowers (see pl. 3). On the side with red lozenges, the interstices are white and embroidered with flowers; on the side with white lozenges, the interstices are red and embroidered with tiny vignettes of rural scenes, each one illustrating some episode in a well-known literary work.

The manner in which the patterning is arranged on this *nuihaku* is called *katamigawari*, meaning "one side differs from the other." This is one of the three types of sectional placement of patterning on *kosode* that was popular in the Momoyama and early Edo period. A second style called *dangawari*, "levels different," is seen on a sixteenth century Momoyama *nuihaku* Nō costume in the Tokyo National Museum (fig. 2). This costume has red and white squares that alternate the length of the fabric. When the fabric lengths were sewn together, a red square was placed next to a white square. These two squares of the same color are never side by side. They are always are at "different levels." Some of the motifs on the Tokyo National Museum's *nuihaku* are similar to those on the Art Institute's *nuihaku*, but the Art Institute's has an almost infinite variety of designs and a richness of detail that gives an impression of no design area in the interstices being repeated. There is a unity of patterning that borders on *sōmoyō*, "a complete design." The many vignettes probably illustrate some ancient story.

The third type of sectional placement of patterning on Momoyama *kosode* is *katasuso*, "shoulders and bottom," meaning that the *kosode* is patterned only in those areas. A sixteenth-century *nuihaku* Nō costume from the Kasuga Shrine, Seki City, Gifu Prefecture (fig. 3) has this type of patterning. This *nuihaku* uses only the two dominant motifs seen on the Art Institute's *nuihaku*—the tiered lozenges, *matsu kawa bishi*, and the willow branches laden with snow, *yuki mochi yanagi*. The elegant simplicity of the design on the Kasuga Shrine *nuihaku* is an interesting contrast to the varied and extremely detailed patterning of the Art Institute's *nuihaku*.

The fabric used for the Art Institute's Monoyama *nuihaku* is called *nerinuki*. To create the patterning of this *nuihaku*, lengths of white *nerinuki* were dyed red in

FIGURE 2. *Nuihaku* (Nō costume), Momoyama period, sixteenth century. Silk. Tokyo National Museum (2904). Photo courtesy of Tokyo National Museum. This *nuihaku* has a design of flowering plants, tanzaku paper, and plank bridges on a red and white checkered ground. A feature of this costume is its *dangawari* ("levels different"), which is the second type of sectional placement of patterning on *kosode*. See pls. 1–3, cat. no. 1, to compare this sixteenth-century Nō costume with the Art Institute's Momoyama *nuihaku*.

Types of Nō Costumes

In terms of style, Nō costumes can be divided into three categories: *kosodemono*, *ōsodemono*, and *hakama*.

The following descriptions of each type of Nō costume are based on Ken Kirihata's listing in his article "Special Features of Noh Costumes."[18] There are various costumes for roles of minor importance, such as the *kitsuke*, that are not listed; many of these costumes are similar to the garments worn in everyday life.

For those costumes represented in The Art Institute of Chicago's collection, the relevant accession, plate, figure, and catalogue numbers are given.

I. *Kosodemono*. *Kosode* with sleeves made of a single width of fabric and having a small opening for the arm. Note: *Kosode* are the garments the Western world calls "kimono." The individual name of each of these *kosodemono* is derived from the name of the fabric used to make the *kosode*. The various types of *kosodemono* are:

karaori	A *kosode* made of warp-float faced 2/1 twill weave with supplementary brocading wefts of long floats that resemble needlework. Worn as an outer robe primarily for female roles. Acc. nos. 1929.92, 1968.142 Pls. 7–8, fig. 6 Cat. nos. 5–6
atsuita	A *kosode* made usually of twill weave but sometimes in plain weave and patterned in supplementary weft floats shorter than those used in *karaori*. The patterning may be simple or it may consist of large motifs in strong colors that are used to create startling contrasts. Worn mainly for male roles.
atsuita karaori	A *kosode* made of an *atsuita* fabric but with a bold patterning woven with the longer supplementary weft floats used for *karaori*. An *atsuita karaori* is used as an under robe for male roles and as an outer robe for female roles. Acc. nos. 1936.149, 1894.66, 1968.143 Pls. 9–11 Cat. nos. 7–9
noshime	A *kosode* worn as an inner robe woven in plain weave that is lustrous or glossy. The patterning is in stripes, *shima*, used either horizontally or in plaids.
surihaku	A *kosode* of either plain weave or a monochromatic figured satin weave, usually either white or red, on which the patterning is created by impressing gold or silver foil on an adhesive that has been applied to the fabric through a stencil. It is an inner robe worn for the role of a woman tormented by a demon. Acc. no. 1928.811

	Pl. 6 Cat. no. 4
nuihaku	A *kosode* of plain weave or satin weave patterned in a combination of needlework and stenciled impressed gold or silver foil. Used mainly for female roles. Worn either as an outer robe or an inner robe. Can be worn in the *koshimaki* manner (see below) over a *surihaku* robe. For a male role, it is an inner robe worn by an emperor, or a noble of high rank, or a youth. Acc. nos. 1928.814, 1964.272, 1930.19 Pls. 1–5 Cat. nos. 1–3
koshimaki	This is both the name of a *kosode* and the manner in which two *kosode* are worn together. The *kosode* can be two *nuihaku*, or an inner *surihaku* and an outer *nuihaku*, or an inner *karaori* and an outer *nuihaku*. The softer and more pliable satin weave outer robe, the *nuihaku*, is folded down at the waist so that the sleeves hang over the hips.

II. *Ōsodemono*. Outer garments with wide sleeves and a large opening for the arm. Some overlap in the front; some do not. The various types of *ōsodemono* are:

chōken	Literally "long silk." A free-falling, unlined dancing cloak usually made of gauze weave fabric. It does not overlap in the front. The front and back panels are attached only at the shoulders. Used mainly for female roles, but can be used for the role of a nobleman. Acc. nos. 1928.812, 1930.101 Pls. 12, 14 Cat. nos. 10–11
maiginu	Literally "dancing silk." An unlined dancing cloak usually made of a gauze weave fabric. It overlaps in the front. The front and back panels are seamed partway down the sides. It is longer than the *chōken* and worn belted. Used for female roles.
mizugoromo	Literally "water cloak." An unlined traveling cloak in a single unpatterned color, or with checked or striped patterning. It is sewn at the sides and overlaps in the front. For both male and female roles.
kariginu	Literally "hunting silk." A round-necked cloak, either unlined or lined. It is unseamed at the sides except where the sleeves are attached to the back. Narrow ornamental cords are threaded through the edges of the sleeves and tied in a knot below the cuff. Worn for the role of a nobleman or a male deity. Acc. no. 1940.1102a

nōshi	Pl. 18 Cat. no. 16 A round-necked cloak very similar to the *kariginu*. On each side at the hemline it has a wide band to hold together the front and back panels, which are not seamed on the sides. It does not have ornamental cords on the sleeves. Originally, it was an informal costume for court nobles. Today *kariginu* are usually substituted for *nōshi*.
happi	A lined or unlined short coat that does not overlap in the front. The front and back panels, which are not seamed on the sides, are held together at the hemline with a wide band in the manner of the *nōshi*. Since *happi* are worn to imitate armor in the roles of military generals, the most favored fabric is *kinran*; sometimes colored silk thread is added to create *nishiki*. The Nō costume *happi* is different from the *happi* worn by commoners.
sobatsugi	A sleeveless version of the *happi*. It also simulates armor but is worn by soldiers, not generals. It is worn also for the roles of Chinese men.
hitatare	A short lined coat similar to the *happi* but with the sides seamed and made of a resist-dyed, patterned hemp fabric. May be worn separately or with matching trousers, *hakama*, as formal military dress, an outfit that is also called *hitatare*. The *hitatare* worn in everyday life by *samurai* and *daimyo* was made of silk.
suō	Identical to the *hitatare* in fabric, method of patterning, and style, but unlined. The coat and trousers are worn for the roles of low-ranking soldiers, village people, etc.

III. *Hakama*. Skirtlike trousers. The various types of *hakama* are:

ōguchi	A plain-colored or patterned skirtlike trouser with large pleats in the front and stiffened panels in the back.
hangiri	A boldly patterned skirtlike trouser resembling the *ōguchi*. While the rear part of the *ōguchi* is made of hard, tightly woven cloth, that of *hangiri* is stiffened with the interlining of woven rush. Acc. nos. 1928.813, 1928.846 Pls. 16–17 Cat. nos. 14–15
sashinuki	Long pleated trousers gathered at the ankles. Worn over *ōguchi*. Acc. no. 1940.1102b Pl. 19 Cat. no. 17

predetermined areas using a dye that was expensive to make. Safflower, *benibana*, petals were used to make this dye. The gathering of a vast number of petals and their processing to make the dye was very time consuming, as were the many times the fabric had to be dipped into the dye to get the desired color. Therefore, only the wealthiest people could afford garments dyed with *beni*, the common name for this safflower dye. The present color of the red areas, a light orangish-red, is the result of fading, which occurs when silk dyed with *beni* is exposed to light. The red areas were originally a bright scarlet.

When the edges of the dyed patterning of this *nuihaku* (pl. 1) were observed under a microscope, no needle holes were seen. Therefore, this patterning was not done by the resist-dyeing technique called *shibori*. When the manner in which the lozenge design is repeated was carefully analyzed, it became obvious that the patterning was produced by the resist-dyeing technique called *itajime*. This is a technique in which the fabric is clamped between two wooden boards on which the pattern is carved. Dye is then poured into the carved-out areas of the boards through previously drilled holes, but the dye cannot penetrate the cloth tightly pressed between the sections of the board that are not carved.[19]

The silk thread in the finest Momoyama and Edo period garments is different from that used in later periods. In researching the fabrics used in Edo period Nō costumes, Akira Yamaguchi has discovered that,

Generally, Edo silk thread had a more beautiful luster and whiteness than the silk of today: it was both finer. . .and exceedingly strong. Silkworms, however, were weak and cocoons so small. . .that they yielded little thread. Further, while there is no way to calculate the twist of thread. . .we may assume it was minimal.[20]

In the earliest methods of hand-reeling the cocoons, there was very little twist in the thread. As more efficient reeling tools were invented, a discernible though slight twist was created in the reeling. The best-quality thread had the least twist and was unwound by hand from cocoons a day or two after they had been spun, while the pupa was still alive within the cocoon. Since this had to be done within a two-week period in the spring before the pupa became a butterfly and broke out of the cocoon, only a relatively small amount of thread could be produced using this method and it was very expensive. Later in the year, the thread taken from cocoons in which the pupa had been killed was not as glossy or resilient.

A textile analysis of the Art Institute's Momoyama *nuihaku* showed that the warp threads in the white undyed areas retain the sericin. The range of colors used in the needlework is limited. It is embroidered in shades of red, yellow, green, blue, purple, and white; only a few

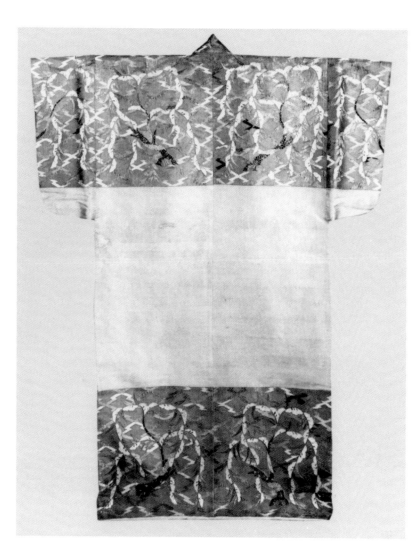

FIGURE 3. *Nuihaku* (Nō costume), Momoyama period, sixteenth century. Silk; needlework; red and light blue *nerinuki* ground. Kasuga Shrine, Seki City, Gifu Prefecture. Photo: Sakai City Museum, *Nui — Decorative Technique in Kosode*, exh. cat. (1987), p. 41, no. 4. This *nuihaku*, which has a pattern of pine-bark lozenges and snow-covered willows, has been designed with the third type of sectional placement of patterning on *kosode*: *katasuso* ("shoulders and bottom"), meaning that it is patterned only in the upper and lower areas of the costume. To compare this type of pattern with that of other *nuihaku*, see fig. 2 and pls. 1–3.

embroidery stitches are used, namely satin, single satin, surface satin, stem stitches, and couching. Outlines of motifs to be embroidered were drawn in black *sumi* ink. The gold foil was impressed over an adhesive that was applied with stencils *after* the needlework was worked. This is evident because minute fragments were left in the embroidery floss when the gold leaf was removed. A few areas were re-embroidered at a later date.[21]

The Art Institute has two other *nuihaku*, one from the middle Edo period with additional needlework added in the late Edo period (pl. 4; fig. 4; cat. no. 2), and another dated late Edo period (pl. 5; fig. 5; cat. no. 3). On the middle Edo period *nuihaku*, the needlework added later was done to make the garment conform to the taste of the late Edo period, when it was fashionable to put as much embellishment as possible into an allotted space.

The late Edo period *nuihaku* was carefully studied and precisely dated by Iwao Nagasaki, who wrote that

this *nuihaku* "displays the premodern style of tightly arranged patterns lacking broad, empty spaces. It is considered to have been made at the beginning of the 19th century, as there exists an equivalent example which bears an inscription of its production date, 1826, and is owned by the Itsukushima Shrine in Hiroshima."[22]

In the needlework of this *nuihaku* there is gold-wrapped thread.[23] Four rows of this thread are laid side-by-side, and couched together, two rows at a time. Such a lavish use of gold-wrapped thread is typical of the period. A flat gold thread is also used in Japanese needlework and weaving. When used in weaving, this gold thread can have the appearance of *surihaku*, which is the technique of pressing thin sheets of gold foil onto a paste applied directly to the fabric. On both of the Edo period *nuihaku kosode*, the *surihaku* technique used with the embroidered motifs was applied after the needlework was completed.

The squares of silver foil on the *surihaku* background of the dark blue satin *nuihaku* (see fig. 4) create a dramatic effect that could well be considered sufficient patterning for a *kosode* without any needlework added. The Nō costume called *surihaku* are patterned with just the impressed gold or silver leaf. The Art Institute's red satin *surihaku kosode* (pl. 6; cat. no. 4) also uses the checkered pattern, *ishidatami*. These squares, however, are only on the skirt and are arranged as lozenges. In contrast, the bodice has a curvilinear design of overlapping waves, *sei-ga-ha*. The *surihaku kosode* is worn as an inner robe, and, if the outer robe is worn *koshimaki* style (see "Types of Nō Costumes"), most of the patterning on the skirt is hidden. The technical analysis of the fabric revealed that the adhesive on which the gold foil is impressed is only lightly sponged on the fabric of the skirt. The gold foil used is quite thin and, when applied on the adhesive, only partly covers the surface of the squares. On the bodice, a thick layer of gold foil is applied over a substantial amount of adhesive.

Karaori kosode are the Nō costumes most often seen in Western collections. As early as the Heian period, *karaori*, meaning "Chinese weaving," was a term used to designate textiles imported from China (Kara). In the fifteenth and sixteenth centuries, sumptuous textiles imported from Ming Dynasty (1368–1644) China were used for Nō costumes. In time, one of these Chinese imported textiles came to be known as *karaori*, and Nō costume *kosode* made of this fabric were also called *karaori*. While the early *karaori* Nō costumes were made of fabrics imported from China, shortly after 1578 the weavers of Kyoto were producing *karaori*, a warp-faced 2/1 twill patterned with long floats of supplementary brocading wefts that resemble needlework stitches. In this weave they were attempting to imitate the needlework of the Momoyama period.

The Art Institute's *karaori* Nō costume (pl. 7; cat. no. 5) is a classic example of a *karaori* patterned with autumn grasses against a background of large red and white squares. The patterning in one square spills over into the adjoining square in a manner typical of the latter half of the eighteenth century. On earlier *kosode* with this type of patterning, the motifs were contained within the square. The red and white squares are created by dyeing the warp threads before weaving them. Weaving done with pre-dyed warp threads is called warp ikat or rung dyeing. The red in the ground weave of this *karaori* is the *iro iri*, "with color," that makes it an appropriate costume for the role of a young woman. The autumn flowers are used either to indicate the season or to evoke a sense of the passage of time.

In this *karaori*, there are, in addition to the silk brocading wefts, flat-gold paper thread brocading wefts bound by the main warps in a 1/2 weft-float faced twill. Akira Yamaguchi described the making of this thread:

In the Edo period, the *washi*, paper used for backing was superior *torinoko* made in Eichizen (Fukui Prefecture); for adhesives they used first class *kudzu* [kuzu, arrowroot] paste

FIGURE 4. *Nuihaku* (Nō costume) (detail of pl. 4), Middle Edo period, eighteenth century; additional patterning added in the Late Edo period, early nineteenth century. Silk, warp-float faced 4/1 satin weave; patterned with impressed gold and silver leaf and embroidered with silk in satin, single satin, and stem stitches; laid work and couching; lined with purple silk, plain weave; 169.6 x 136.1 cm. The Art Institute of Chicago, S. M. Nickerson Fund (1964.272). See cat. no. 2.

from Kumagawa in Wakasa (Fukui Prefecture), and lacquer from Eichizen. The gold was beaten into foil by hand and was fairly thick. Since the paper was also cut by hand, the resultant strips were not of strictly uniform widths.[24]

The other *karaori kosode* (pl. 8; cat. no. 6) also has a 2/1 warp-faced twill ground weave in checkered ikat squares but the colors are reddish brown and blue, *iro nashi*, "without color," meaning no bright red, and are appropriate for the role of an older woman. The brocading wefts that create the patterning of water plants are in subdued colors such as yellow-green, green, three shades of blue, two of purple, two of brown, off-white, and white. The ground weave is almost entirely covered with horizontal rows of water plants broken at intervals with a stylized trailing mist in flat gold paper thread to relieve the austerity of the color scheme.

The Art Institute has three *atsuita karaori kosode* (pls. 9–11; cat. nos. 7–9). All of them are patterned in long weft brocading floats that resemble needlework. The motifs are very large and repeated over and over in closely-spaced horizontal rows. They could be worn as an outer robe for the role of a woman of strong character or as an under robe for a male role.

The textile called *atsuita* is a stiff, heavily patterned fabric. Its name is derived from the thick board, called *atsuita*, around which this fabric was rolled when it was imported from China in the sixteenth century. The Nō costume *atsuita* is made from this type of fabric. At Nishijin in Kyoto during the second half of the seventeenth century, the weavers began to weave *atsuita* patterned with the long supplementary weft brocading floats used for *karaori*. The *atsuita karaori* costumes in the collection of the Art Institute are made of this type of fabric.[25] Today some textile authorities call this fabric *karaori*.

The variation in the subtle colors of the checkered background within the large ikat dyed squares of the *atsuita karaori* (see pl. 9) is as important a part of the aesthetic appeal of the patterning as the large motifs. The motifs used for the patterned background of both *karaori* and *atsuita karaori* are usually geometric motifs based on the traditional Heian *yūsoku* patterns of Japanese court costumes. Over the centuries, these motifs have acquired symbolic meanings usually relating to prosperity, wealth, or some desirable personal attribute. They may be chosen because they express a sentiment compatible with that expressed by the larger motifs.

Another Nō costume (pl. 10) is patterned with flower carts against a geometrically patterned background. *Kosode* with this patterning can be found among *karaori* and *atsuita karaori* Nō costumes. To positively identify a Nō robe as *atsuita karaori*, it is necessary to know the role for which the actor chooses to wear it. The patterning of another *atsuita karaori* costume (pl. 11) is very unusual and possibly inappropriate for a Nō costume because it has motifs associated with wedding cere-

FIGURE 5. *Nuihaku* (Nō costume) (detail of pl. 5), Late Edo period, early nineteenth century. Silk, warp-float faced 7/1 satin weave; patterned with impressed gold leaf and embroidered with silk and gold-leaf-paper-strip-wrapped cotton in satin and single satin stitches; laid work and couching; lined with red silk, plain weave; dyed with *beni*, safflower, now faded to orange; 175.1 x 137.5 cm. The Art Institute of Chicago, Restricted gift of Mrs. Clyde M. Carr (1930.19). See cat. no. 3.

FIGURE 6. *Karaori* (Nō costume) (detail of pl. 8), Late Edo period, late eighteenth–early nineteenth century. Silk and gold-leaf-paper strips, warp ikat, warp-float faced 2/1 twill weave with supplementary brocading wefts; lined with blue silk, plain weave, probably a replacement; 162.8 x 133.2 cm. The Art Institute of Chicago, Gift of Mrs. Robert D. Graff (1968.142). See cat. no. 6.

mony rituals. There are the *origami*, folded-paper butter-flies, the male butterfly, *ōchō,* and the female but-terfly, *mechō.* In spite of this unorthodox patterning, this *kosode* is tailored as a Nō costume.

The *chōken*, an unlined patterned gauze weave cloak with very wide sleeves, is a very graceful dancing garment worn mainly in female roles or for the role of a courtier to express his refined elegance. The Art Institute has two *chōken.* Usually a *chōken* is patterned with widely scat-tered "palace motifs," *gosho mon,* that may refer to a classical story. On eighteenth-century *chōken*, the indi-vidual motifs on both the back and front at the chest and shoulder level are large, with much smaller motifs that are sometimes a variation of the larger motif on the skirt and the lower part of the sleeves. The Art Institute's *chōken* are later. One of these *chōken* (pl. 12; cat. no. 10) has an all-over pattern of large fan papers across the top of the cloak from which fall trailing vines of *fuyu aoi* in a manner similar to early twentieth-century *kosode* patterning.

To weave gauze requires great skill, and the complex weave of the white *chōken* (pl. 12) and the Art Institute's other *chōken* (pl. 14; cat. no. 11) are both *tours de force* of the weaving art. This red swastika-patterned gauze *chōken* has the same large motif or a mirror image of it scattered over the entire garment. It is a motif similar to that seen on mid-nineteenth-century *obi.* This *chōken* has been retailored and a lining has been added at a later date. The cords that add weight to the sleeve ends are

missing from both of these *chōken*.

The Art Institute has two patterned gauze weave costumes (pls. 13 and 15; cat. nos. 12–13) that are not tailored to conform with any of the wide-sleeved outer Nō costumes. The length of each garment approximates that of the *maiginu* and both overlap in the front as does a *maiginu.* The sides are not seamed and there are bands on each side at the hemline to hold together the open sides. These two features are characteristic of the Nō *happi* (see "Types of Nō Costumes"). The *happi,* however, does not overlap in the front and is a shorter garment. Although these garments came into the Art Institute's collection as Nō costumes, it is impossible to assign them to any specific style of Nō costume. It is possible that they are an outer summer garment worn by the warrior class on a ceremonial occasion.

The flat gold-paper thread used in the patterning of these costumes (pls. 13 and 15) is unusual because it has gold foil on *both sides* of the paper core. On darker gauze weave costumes, the glow of the gold-paper thread through the gauze weave would give an added sheen to the fabric. Researchers who have examined hundreds of Nō costumes say they have never seen this type of gold thread on a Nō costume.

Hakama, skirtlike trousers, are tailored in many different styles. Each style has its special name. The *ōguchi* and the *hangiri* both have stiffened fabric at the back, but the *hangiri* is stiffened with an interlining of woven reeds.[26] The Art Institute's white satin weave *han-*

FIGURE 7. *Uchikake* (detail of pl. 23). Late Edo–Early Meiji period, nineteenth century. Silk, warp-float faced 4/1 satin weave; embroidered with silk in satin, single satin, and stem stitches; laid work, couching, and Chinese knots; painted with gold; lined with red silk *chirimen*, crepe; dyed with *beni*, safflower; 194.2 x 126.7 cm. The Art Institute of Chicago, Anonymous gift (1958.756). See cat. no. 20.

giri (pl. 16; cat. no. 14) is patterned with plum blossoms floating on water. This patterning is very similar to that of an eighteenth-century *ōguchi* in the Tokyo National Museum with a design of chrysanthemums floating on water. The patterning on the red satin weave *hangiri* (pl. 17; cat. no. 15) is of clouds and the sacred wheel, *rimbō*. This is the type of *yōsoku* motif patterning usually found on *hangiri*. On the underside of the *hangiri* fabric in areas where there is no gold thread in the patterning, there are bound white strips of paper thread without gold foil to maintain the consistent texture and weight of the fabric.

In 1940, the Art Institute acquired as a single gift three pieces of a costume worn for the role of a courtier: an *awase kariginu*, a round-necked lined outer coat fashioned after the Heian hunting cloak; *sashinuki*, pleated trousers gathered and tied at the ankles; and a *koshi obi*, the sash used to adjust the length of the *kariginu* (pls. 18–20; cat. nos. 16–18). The *koshi obi* is the only Nō costume accessory in the Art Institute's collection. It should not be confused with the narrower embroidered headbands, *kazura obi*, that cover the cords that hold the mask in place.

A Kyōgen is an informal play performed without masks. It supplies comic relief to offset the austere, concentrated, emotion-charged atmosphere of the Nō play that precedes it and the one that will follow. The story usually involves a humorous conflict between the master, a member of the lesser nobility, and his servants. The Art Institute's two-piece Kyōgen costume, a *kamishimo* (pls. 21–22; cat. no. 19) would have been worn over a *noshime* (see "Types of Nō Costumes") by the master. The inappropriate fabric used for the *kamishimo* is an unspoken comment on the provincialism of the master and suggests his social ambitions that will lead him eventually into various humorous situations. This all-over pattern of dragons amidst stylized clouds is a classic design reserved for garments of great dignity such as Buddhist priests' robes, *kesa*, or the outer coat, *dōbuku*, worn by the highest military officials. The silk and cotton fabric of which this *kamishimo* is made is patterned with a comic version of this classic design.

Other Japanese Costumes in the Art Institute

In the Western world, the casual observer of Japanese costumes, seeing only the general appearance of the outer garments, calls most of them "kimono." To the Japanese people, "kimono" means simply "clothing." As with Western costume, each Japanese garment has a specific name depending upon subtle variations in styling and color or whether it is worn for a special occasion or in a certain manner.

The word *kosode*, which specifically designates a full-length robe with a shorter sleeve that has a small opening for the arm, has also come to be used as a generic term. The Tokyo National Museum divides its "*kosode* dress" into *kosode*, *furisode*, *uchikake*, *koshimaki*, *kata-bira*, *hitoe*, *aigi*, *ubugi*, and *yogi*.[27]

The Art Institute has four types of "*kosode* dress": *uchikake*, *furisode*, *aigi*, and *kosode*. Each of these *kosode* was originally a length of plain or damask woven white silk fabric. When various lengths of the white silk were sewn into a *kosode*, it became "a painter's canvas," on which the designer outlined his "picture." The *kosode* was then taken apart and various textile artists would execute this "picture" with dyes, needlework stitches, and painting. Since so many "artists" were involved in the creation of these works of art, they were not signed.

Even as the Nō actor's selection of his costume was made according to certain accepted rules regarding its use, women had to select their items of dress according to their age, social position, marital status, and the occasion on which a garment would be worn. Bright colors and elaborate patterning were the privilege of the young. Until married, a girl wore the long, swinging sleeves of the *furisode* and, after marriage, the shorter sleeves of the *kosode*. Economics and social practices controlled the use of luxurious fabrics expensively patterned. These were reserved for the upper classes. The use of certain motifs also indicated the social status of the wearer, such as the *yūsoku* motifs or objects and scenes from literary sources that revealed the wearer's intellectual accomplishments.

In the introductory section on symbolism, the development of the Japanese idea of beauty, *wayō*, in textile design was discussed. This aesthetic is foremost in *kosode* design. Tomoyuki Yamanobe, in discussing the development of the "variety in patterning and delicacy of expression" of *fukusa* design, wrote that in the Edo period the *fukusa* had many similarities to *kosode*: "They both

FIGURE 8. *Furisode* (detail of pl. 25). Late Edo period, nineteenth century. Silk, 4/1 satin damask weave, *rinzu*; *ōbōshi shibori* and embroidered with silk and gold-leaf-paper-strip-wrapped silk, in satin stitches; couching; lined in red silk, plain weave; dyed with *beni*, safflower; 182.8 x 127.7 cm. The Art Institute of Chicago, Gift of Gaylord Donnelley in memory of Frances Gaylord Smith (1991.636). See cat. no. 22.

developed together at a time when the *kosode* reached its high point. That is to say, both have pictorial patterns with an asymmetrical realistic quality based on nature. The contemplation of nature has been part of the Japanese aesthetic from ancient times."[28]

Most *kosode* are worn belted with a sash, an *obi*. The Art Institute is fortunate in having an *uchikake* (pl. 23; fig. 7; cat. no. 20) that is worn as an outer coat without an *obi*. The very large *fuki*, an extension at the hemline of the lining covering a thickly padded roll, weighted the *uchikake* so that it trailed gracefully over the *tatami* matted floor. The delicate needlework illustrating scenes from the *The Tale of Genji* would be destroyed if an *obi* were wrapped around it. The light blue color, the patterning, and the long, swinging sleeves of a *furisode* indicate that this *uchikake* is a garment for a young unmarried woman.

The Art Institute has four other *furisode*. Three of these would be worn with the left side folded over the right side and held in place with an *obi*. The fourth may be an *uchikake*. All are made of *rinzu*, a satin damask weave. Extremely skillful yuzen dyeing was used to create the patterning on the first of these *furisode* (pl. 24; fig. 1; cat. no. 21) At various times in the dyeing process, areas to remain white were kept from absorbing the dyes by applying a paste resist by hand. A paper cone was used to apply free-hand the paste used to resist the white lines of the tree. The resist paste that created the imitation tie-dyeing, *surihitta*, used for some of the *tachibana*, mandarin oranges, was applied to the cloth through the stencils. Many other stencils were used for the grain of the cypress wood of the fan guards and in some background details of the scenes from *The Tale of Genji*. These scenes and other areas were hand-painted with dyes. Then all these patterned areas were covered with another resist paste and the brown background dye was brushed on. After all the paste was removed by immersing the fabric in running water, the needlework was added and additional details painted in *sumi* ink.

The motifs in the patterning of this *furisode* (pl. 24) express wishes for a long and prosperous life. The *tachibana* tree is an auspicious symbol of longevity, and the unfolding cypress fans, *hiōgi*, suggest ever-expanding prosperity. These fans carried by Heian courtiers were chosen as an appropriate motif on which to display scenes from *The Tale of Genji*. These scenes of the cultural attainments of Genji express a wish that the wearer of the *furisode* may continue to live a life of equal refinement. The shorter sleeves of this *furisode*, the darker background, and the rather subdued coloring of the patterning make it appropriate for an older person.

The patterning of clouds and scattered *aoi* leaves on another *furisode* (pl. 25; fig. 8; cat. no. 22) is very simple when compared with the intricate designs on the brown *furisode* discussed above. When the edges of the red clouds are examined under a microscope, there are none of the needle holes required for the running stitches necessary for the most common type of the resist-dyeing technique called *shibori*. The dyed areas were created by a more difficult type of *shibori*, *ōboshi shibori*. The fabric was gathered together with the fingers against a circular disk inserted beneath the fabric; then the gathers were held in place by wrapping string around the disk. The cloth not to be dyed was resisted by covering it with bamboo husks. For example, the red areas were dyed, while the rest of the fabric was covered with the bamboo husk. Then the red areas were covered with bamboo husk resist and the blue areas were dyed. When the dyeing was completed very fine undyed white lines were left between the red and blue areas, and these were covered with couched gold-wrapped thread.

The informal pairs of this type of *aoi*, asarum, leaves in the patterning of this *furisode* (pl. 25) suggests that it would have belonged to a member of one of the branches of the Tokugawa family that had been awarded the privilege of using a crest, *mon*, of paired thirteen-veined *aoi* leaves.[29] In the Edo period, upper-class families sometimes incorporated their crest into the patterning of a textile. In the late Edo or early Meiji period, the family crest was placed on the center back, the back of the sleeves, and on the chest at the left and right sides of the garment. At this time, the common people also began to use a family crest in this manner.

The realistically drawn blossoming plum tree on the red *furisode* (pl. 26; fig. 9; cat. no. 23) is yet another type of *furisode* patterning. The carefully delineated picture of a tree embroidered from shoulder to hemline on the back of this *furisode* shows the influence of Western art on Japanese design. Needlework typical of this period was used to portray realistically the contours of the tree trunk. First the edges of the trunk were padded with a heavy thread and, over this padding, gold-wrapped thread was couched with red silk thread.

This *furisode* belonged to a family whose crest was the *tachibana*. Since these large crests are placed as described above, this *furisode* would be worn on formal occasions, probably as an *uchikake*, an outer coat worn without an *obi*. An *obi* worn over this *furisode* would interrupt the flow of the patterning.

Another use of the family crest is seen on an *aigi* (pl. 27; cat. no. 24). *Aigi* are full-length *kosode* worn under an *uchikake* and are usually patterned by *kanoko*, "fawn spot," tie-dying. Here the large tie-dyed design of tea plant fruit crests, *chanomi mon*, are scattered over the flowing water design, called Kanze *mizu*. Iwao Nagasaki wrote, "This stylized design of flowing water is said to

FIGURE 9. *Furisode* (detail of pl. 26). Late Edo period, nineteenth century. Silk, 4/1 satin damask weave, *rinzu*; embroidered with silk and gold-leaf-paper-wrapped silk, in satin stitches; laid work, couching, and padded couching; lined in red silk, plain weave; dyed with *beni*, safflower; 183.8 x 128.8 cm. The Art Institute of Chicago, Gift of Gaylord Donnelley in memory of Frances Gaylord Smith (1991.637). See cat. no. 23.

have originated with the *kanze* sect of the Noh theater."[30] Kanze *mizu* is a motif used in the patterning of textiles on colored woodcut prints.

The Art Institute is fortunate in having three winter *kosode* because they are garments seldom found in collections. Two still have their inner padding of silk floss. The source of this wadding, *mawata*, is the pierced cocoons, *degara*, from which the moth has emerged.[31] After being soaked, the pierced cocoon can be stretched into a large flat square. The tenth print in a series of woodcuts by Utamaro entitled *Women's Work in Silk Culture* (*Joshoku kaiko tewaza gusa*) shows women stretching this waste silk floss on wooden posts (see, in this issue, James T. Ulak, "Utamaro's Views of Sericulture," fig. 7c).

The patterning of the woven fabrics used to make these winter *kosode* provides a brief glimpse of the eighteenth-century skills of the Nishijin weavers of Kyoto. The fabrics used for these winter *kosode* also would have been used for *kesa*, the Japanese priest's mantle, usually considered a robe.

One of the winter *kosode* (pl. 29; cat. no. 25) has an all-over pattern of rows of large clusters of fanciful fruits and flowers. This pattern may be a late eighteenth-century Japanese version of the Western bizarre-type silks woven in Europe in the early eighteenth century. The lining of this *kosode* is missing, but it still has an interlining.

Another winter *kosode* (pl. 30; fig. 10; cat. no. 26) has an all-over pattern of dragons chasing the sacred jewel amidst clouds. This pattern "was invented in China

FIGURE 10. *Kosode* (detail of pl. 30). Late Edo period, late eighteenth century. Silk and gold-leaf-paper-strip-wrapped cotton, warp-float faced 4/1 satin weave with supplementary patterning wefts; lined with red silk *chirimen*, crepe; dyed with *beni*, safflower; with an interlining of lightly wadded *mawata*, floss; 180.5 x 125.8 cm. The Art Institute of Chicago, Gift of Mrs. Robert D. Graff (1957.154). See cat. no. 26.

about 1600 and. . .introduced into Japan by way of Ezo (Hokkaido) and other northern provinces."[32] The history of this fabric is an interesting example of how inaccuracies concerning an imported fabric originated in a period when traveling was difficult. As recently as 1914, this type of fabric was called Yezo (i.e. Ezo) *nishiki*, "Produced at In-u, one of the Northern Provinces of Japan. Pattern: Banreki-Ryu (celebrated Ming pattern of dragons)."[33] One version of this pattern was incorrectly assumed to have been "copied from an original Ainu design."[34] The Japanese version of this pattern, called Ezo *nishiki*, was considered one of the most prized productions of the Nishijin looms during the Edo period. This fabric was especially prized for campaign coats, *jinbaori*, for a general; *kesa* for high-ranking Buddhist monks; and temple furnishings. There are many variations on this pattern, including a humorous one used for the Art Institute's *kamishimo* (pl. 22), a Kyōgen costume, in which the

dragons searching amidst the clouds seem unable to find the sacred jewels.

The third padded winter garment is actually a *furisode* (pl. 28; cat. no. 27). The ground wefts of this fabric are strips of narrow, flat gold-paper thread of various widths, which means they were cut by hand, not by machine. They were inserted one at a time and pulled from selvage to selvage by a hooked bamboo stick. Against this plain weave background with its soft, almost indiscernible golden glow, supplementary patterning weft floats weave undulating trunks of blooming plum trees. Although it is difficult to believe that this fabric was woven on a draw loom without a Jacquard attachment, this device did not come to Japan until 1873. Both the patterning and the technical analysis of the gold paper indicate an eighteenth-century date.

The Art Institute has both a woman's *haori* and a man's *haori*, which are informal three-quarter-length outer coats. *Haori* are lined to the waist with a patterned fabric. The black plain weave fabric of the woman's *haori* (pl. 31; cat. no. 28) gives no hint of the luxurious pink satin weave lining patterned with clematis, *tessen*, and scrolling vines and leaves in a spiraling meander, *karakusa*, literally "Chinese grasses." These patterns, sometimes called arabesques, have hardly changed since the eighth century.

The man's *haori* (pl. 32; cat. no. 29) is one of the finest pieces of weaving among the garments discussed in this article. It is plain weave double cloth (see Glossary). It has been woven with two different patterns. Most of this *haori* is woven in a wavy pattern resembling ikat, but an area extending from the chest to the hip line is an extremely fine lattice pattern, *mijin gōshi*.

Nō robes for the most dignified characters have lattices on which the horizontal stripes predominate. On the outside of this *haori*, the strips are vertical, but inside on the lining, known only to the wearer, there are bold horizontal strips. Perhaps a sly symbolism exists in the patterning of this *haori*. In the Nō drama *Okina*, the old man wears a *noshime*, an under robe, with the top and bottom of a plain color but with a lattice pattern, *Okina gōshi*, around the waist, which is just barely visible under the *kariginu*. Although the lattice pattern, *mijin gōshi*, on this twentieth-century *haori* is not the *Okina gōshi* lattice, it may have been chosen for this *haori* because the wearer was a devotee of the Nō drama. If so, he would understand that it conveyed a prayer for good fortune and happiness, just like the Nō dance of the sacred elderly man, Okina. Possibly this warm padded *haori* was a gift to an elderly man at the New Year.

Catalogue

Nō Drama Costumes and Other Japanese Costumes in the Collection of The Art Institute of Chicago

A glossary appears on pages 95–100.

The catalogue entries are in the following order: Nō costumes, a Kyōgen costume, *kosode*, and *haori*.

Figure numbers indicate where illustrations of particular garments appear in Mary V. Hays and Ralph E. Hays, "Nō Drama Costumes and Other Japanese Costumes in The Art Institute of Chicago," pp. 20–36.

Nō costumes by type:

1. *Nuihaku* (**Nō costume**), Momoyama period, sixteenth century. Pls. 1–3.

Silk, plain weave; patterned with *itajime*, impressed gold leaf and embroidered with silk in satin, single satin, surface satin, and stem stitches; couching. The interstices of the bold lozenge motifs called *matsu kawa bishi*, the pine-bark lozenge, have vignettes of scenes recognizable as literary references and still-life compositions of various plants and flowers. The flowers and scenes depicted have symbolic implications with numerous wishes for good fortune. A few areas have been re-embroidered at a later date. Lined with red silk, plain weave; dyed with *beni*, safflower, now faded to orange.

160.6 x 133.1 cm; 63¼ x 52⅜ in.

Restricted gift of Mrs. C. H. Worcester, 1928.814

This *nuihaku* was altered at a later date to conform to the style of that era. Fragments of another Momoyama *nuihaku* were used for an extra outer panel on each sleeve and at the hemline to lengthen the robe and to create the points at the front of the hemline. The patterning of this fabric is "fan papers" and flowers (see pls. 2–3 for details).

2. *Nuihaku* (**Nō costume**), Middle Edo period, eighteenth century. Additional patterning added in the Late Edo period, early nineteenth century. Pl. 4, fig. 4.

Silk, warp-float faced 4/1 satin weave; patterned with impressed gold and silver leaf and embroidered with silk in satin, single satin, and stem stitches; laid work and couching. Lined with purple silk, plain weave.

169.6 x 136.1 cm; 66¾ x 53⅝ in.

S. M. Nickerson Fund, 1964.272

Originally the design on this robe consisted of the all-over checkered design, *ishidatami*, and the embroidered fans, a repeated crest, *mon*, and rectangular poem papers, *tanzaku*. In the nineteenth century, a spiral thread made of silk floss Z-plied was couched down the center of the poem papers and around their edges, transforming them into planks. Embroidered iris and water currents were added to create a vignette that illustrates the Yatsuhashi chapter of *The Tales of Ise*, which takes place near a plank bridge in eight sections surrounded by blooming iris.

3. *Nuihaku* (**Nō costume**), Late Edo period, early nineteenth century. Pl. 5, fig. 5.

Silk, warp-float faced 7/1 satin weave; patterned with impressed gold leaf and embroidered with silk and gold-leaf-paper-strip-wrapped cotton in satin and single satin stitches; laid work and couching. Lined with red silk, plain weave; dyed with *beni*, safflower, now faded to orange.

175.1 x 137.5 cm; 68⅞ x 54⅛ in.

Restricted gift of Mrs. Clyde M. Carr, 1930.19

After the roundels were embroidered, the adhesive for the impressed gold leaf was applied through a stencil around the needlework in the center of the roundels.

4. *Surihaku* (**Nō costume**), Late Edo period, late eighteenth–early nineteenth century. Pl. 6.

Silk, warp-float faced 7/1 satin weave; patterned with impressed gold leaf. Lined with red silk, plain weave; dyed with *beni*, safflower.

173.1 x 137.2 cm; 68⅛ x 54 in.

Restricted gift of Robert Allerton, 1928.811

The skirt of the robe is patterned with an all-over, checkered design, *ishidatami*, and the bodice is patterned with a stylized, curvilinear design of overlapping waves, *sei-ga-ha*.

5. *Karaori* (**Nō costume**), Middle to Late Edo period, eighteenth century. Pl. 7.

Silk and gold-leaf-paper strips, warp ikat, warp-float faced 2/1 twill weave with supplementary brocading wefts. The long silk weft patterning floats resemble needlework. Lined with red silk, plain weave; dyed with *beni*, safflower, now faded to orange.

171.4 x 136.5 cm; 67½ x 53¾ in.

Restricted gift of Otto C. Deering, 1929.92

The checkered warp ikat ground is patterned with five of the Seven Plants of Autumn: chrysanthemum, *kiku*; valerian, *ominaeshi*; balloon flower, *kikyō*; bush clover, *hagi*; and eulalia, *susuki*.

6. *Karaori* (**Nō costume**), Late Edo period, late eighteenth–early nineteenth century. Pl. 8, fig. 6.

Silk and gold-leaf-paper strips, warp ikat, warp-float faced 2/1 twill weave with supplementary brocading wefts. The long floats resemble needlework. Lined with blue silk, plain weave, probably a replacement.

162.8 x 133.2 cm; 64 x 52½ in.

Gift of Mrs. Robert D. Graff, 1968.142

CAT. NO. 2

The checkered warp ikat ground is patterned with water *aoi*, *mizu aoi*, and candocks, *kōhone*, alternately arranged in rows. Each row is divided by *kasumi*, a stylized trailing mist.

7. *Atsuita karaori* (Nō costume), Late Edo period, late eighteenth century. Pl. 9.

Silk and gold-leaf-paper strips, warp ikat, warp-float faced 2/1 twill weave with supplementary patterning and brocading wefts. Lined with white silk, plain weave.

168.2 x 146.3 cm; 66¼ x 57⅝ in.

Gift of Natalie Gookin in memory of Frederick W. Gookin, 1936.149

The large ikat dyed squares have a background pattern of a checkered design, *ishidatami*. Brocaded over each square in long weft floats is a large spray of balloon flowers, *kikyō*, and a folded paper, *noshi*, a *hanahoshi*, filled with chrysanthemums, *kiku*, and eulalia, *susuki*, leaves.

8. *Atsuita karaori* (Nō costume), Late Edo period, early nineteenth century. Pl. 10.

Silk and gold-leaf-paper strips, warp-float faced 2/1 twill weave with supplementary patterning wefts. Lined with red silk, plain weave; dyed with *beni*, safflower, now faded to orange.

176.4 x 144.5 cm; 69½ x 56⅞ in.

Gift of the Antiquarian Society of The Art Institute of Chicago, 1894.66

The ground is patterned with an all-over "seven treasures," *shippō*, fret of interlocking circles against which are flower carts filled with two types of chrysanthemums, *kiku*, and balloon flowers, *kikyō*.

9. *Atsuita karaori* (Nō costume), Late Edo period, early nineteenth century. Pl. 11.

Silk and gold-leaf-paper strips, warp-float faced 2/1 twill weave with supplementary brocading wefts. Lined with red silk, plain weave; dyed with *beni*, safflower, now faded to orange.

172.8 x 136.9 cm; 68 x 53⅞ in.

Gift of Mrs. Robert D. Graff, 1968.143

The ground is patterned with an all-over hemp leaf, *asa no ha*, fret against which are two types of folded "paper" butterflies, *chōhanagata*—a male butterfly, *ōchō*, and a female butterfly, *mechō*—and large cherry blossoms, *sakura*. Although tailored as a Nō robe, the patterning is unusual and possibly inappropriate because there are motifs for a wedding *uchikake*.

10. *Chōken* (Nō costume), Late Meiji–Early Taisho period, early twentieth century. Pl. 12.

Silk and gold-leaf-paper strips, complex gauze weave with supplementary brocading wefts. Unlined.

124.5 x 207 cm; 49 x 81½ in.

Restricted gift of Mrs. J. L. Valentine, 1928.812

The patterning in flat gold-paper thread is a large "fan paper," out of which fall trailing vines of flowering *fuyu aoi*, an asarum lily.

11. *Chōken* (Nō costume), Late Edo period, mid-nineteenth century. Pl. 14.

Silk and gold-leaf-paper strips, complex gauze weave with supplementary brocading wefts and self-patterned by areas of twill interlacing. Lined with red silk, plain weave; dyed with *beni*, safflower. This garment normally would have had no lining.

110 x 199.5 cm; 43¼ x 78½ in.

Restricted gift of the Orientals; Nickerson Fund, 1930.101

CAT. NO. 7

The gauze has a *sayagata* pattern, a diaper of interlocking swastikas. On this background is brocaded in flat gold-paper two different designs that use the same motifs of five of the Seven Plants of Autumn, *Aki no nanakusa*, a butterfly, *chō*, and a May fly, *kanedo*. The five flowers depicted are: chrysanthemum, *kiku*; eulalia, *susuki*; bush clover, *hagi*; balloon flower, *kikyō*; and valerian, *ominaeshi*.

12. Unusual *ōsodemono*-style garment. Possibly not a Nō costume. Late Edo period, early nineteenth century. Pl. 13.

Silk and gold-leaf-paper strips, complex gauze weave with supplementary brocading wefts. Unlined. The gold-leaf-paper strips have gold leaf on both sides of the paper. This costume does not conform to the prescribed tailoring of any particular Nō costume. It may be a summer outer garment worn for ceremonial occasions by someone of the warrior class.

132.2 x 218.6 cm; 52 x 86⅛ in.

Restricted gift of the Orientals, 1930.100

Loosely coiled cloud motifs with short, undulating tails.

13. Unusual *ōsodemono*-style garment. Possibly not a Nō costume. Meiji period, late nineteenth century. Pl. 15.

Silk and gold-leaf-paper strips, complex gauze weave with supplementary brocading wefts. Unlined. The gold-leaf-paper strips have gold leaf on both sides of the paper. This costume may be a summer outer garment for a member of the warrior class.

138.5 x 228.8 cm; 54½ x 87¾ in.

Restricted gift of Frank G. Logan, 1928.810

Pictorial motifs of lotus growing out of the water.

14. *Hangiri* (Nō costume), Late Edo period, early nineteenth century. Pl. 16.

Silk and gold-leaf-paper strips, warp-float faced 7/1 satin weave with plain interlacings of secondary binding warps and supplementary patterning wefts. Lined with purple silk, plain weave. The back of this garment is stiffened with an interlining of woven reeds; when the plaited cords are tightened and tied, they give the stiffened back a slightly circular contour. The trousers are held in place by being wrapped and tied around the waist by the two long, narrow sashes.

108.9 x 79 cm (at waist); 42⅞ x 31⅞ in. (at waist)

Restricted gift of Robert Allerton, 1928.813

The satin woven silk is patterned with a design of plum blossoms floating on turbulent waters.

15. *Hangiri* (**Nō costume**), Meiji period, late nineteenth century. Pl. 17.

Silk and gold-leaf-paper strips, warp-float faced 7/1 satin weave with plain interlacing of secondary binding warps and supplementary patterning wefts. Lined with purple silk, plain weave. The back of this garment is stiffened with an interlining of woven reeds.

105.8 x 75 cm (at waist); 41⅝ x 29½ in. (at waist)

Gift of Alfred Hamill, 1928.846

Against a background of loosely coiled clouds are large motifs of the sacred wheel, *rimbō*. *Hangiri* are often worn with *happi*.

16. *Awase kariginu* (**Nō costume**), Late Edo–Early Meiji period, nineteenth century. Pl. 18.

Silk, complex gauze weave self-patterned by areas of plain interlacing. Lined with white silk, plain weave. A distinctive feature of the *kariginu* is the narrow woven tape threaded through the edge of the sleeve, with the end artistically knotted and falling below the sleeve.

96.5 x 148.6 cm; 38 x 58½ in.

Oriental Department Sundry Trust, 1940.1102a

The gauze weave is patterned with *fusenryō*, floral roundels, based on *yūsoku*, literally "ancient court," patterning.

17. *Sashinuki* (**Nō costume**), Late Edo–Early Meiji period, nineteenth century. Pl. 19.

Silk, weft-ribbed plain weave. Unlined. These trousers are worn gathered at the ankles by drawing together and tying the plaited cords inserted in the hem.

165.1 x 33 cm (at waist); 65 x 13 in. (at waist)

Oriental Department Sundry Trust, 1940.1102b

The white fabric in the crotch and at the center front indicates that this *sashinuki* was worn under a *hangiri* or *ōguchi*.

18. *Koshi obi*, sash, used to adjust the outer garment of a Nō costume, Late Meiji period, late nineteenth or early twentieth century. Pl. 20.

Silk, warp ikat, warp-faced, weft-ribbed plain weave; embroidered with silk in satin, stem, and straight stitches. The band to hold it in place is woven in plain weave.

Decorated sash: 65 x 9.2 cm; 25 x 3⅝ in.
Band: 240 x 8 cm; 94⅝ x 3⅛ in.

Oriental Department Sundry Trust, 1940.1102c,d

The band passes through the sash and is then secured around the waist. This gives the appearance of a long, decorated sash. The *koshi obi* is used to adjust the length of an outer robe or jacket.

The sash is embroidered with the formal crest, *mon*, of the Tokugawa family. Between this crest of three *aoi*, asarum, leaves are the informal imperial crests of the paulownia tree, *kiri*, and phoenix, *hō-ō*.

Kyōgen costume:

19. *Kamishimo* (**Kyōgen costume**), Showa period, first half of the twentieth century. Pls. 21–22.

The jacket and trousers are of silk, cotton and gold-leaf-paper strips, warp-float faced 5/1 twill weave woven with twill interlacings of secondary binding warps and supplementary patterning wefts. The jacket is lined with blue silk, warp-float faced 3/1 twill weave. The trousers are lined with white plain weave woven in silk and cotton.

Jacket: 87.3 x 90.2 cm; 34⅜ x 35½ in.
Trousers: 113 x 18.2 cm (at waist); 44½ x 7⅛ in. (at waist)

Bequest of Mrs. Herman J. Hall, 1933.918b,c

A *kamishimo*, literally "upper and lower," consists of two garments. The "upper" is the *kataginu*, literally "the silk covering the shoulders." The "lower" is the *hakama*, the trousers. Both the *kataginu* and the *hakama* are patterned with an all-over design of dragons amidst clouds.

***Kosode* by type:**

20. *Uchikake*, Late Edo–Early Meiji period, nineteenth century. Pl. 23, fig. 7.

Silk, warp-float faced 4/1 satin weave; embroidered with silk in satin, single satin, and stem stitches; laid work, couching, and Chinese knots; painted with gold. Lined with red silk *chirimen*, crepe; dyed with *beni*, safflower.

194.2 x 126.7 cm; 76½ x 49⅞ in.

Anonymous gift, 1958.756

The embroidered motifs relate to the fifty-four chapters of *The Tale of Genji*. The crest, *mon*, is an orchid, *ran*.

21. *Furisode*, Late Edo period, nineteenth century. Pl. 24, fig. 1.

Silk, 4/1 satin damask weave, *rinzu*; yuzen dyed, painted, stenciled, and embroidered with silk and gold-leaf-paper-strip-wrapped cotton in satin and single-satin stitches; laid work, couching, and Chinese knots. Lined with red silk, plain weave; dyed with *beni*, safflower.

183.7 x 122.7 cm; 72⅜ x 48⅜ in.

Gift of Gaylord Donnelley in memory of Frances Gaylord Smith, 1991.635

The *rinzu* has a pattern of a *sayagata* fret of swastikas over which is scattered a motif of either an individual orchid or a chrysanthemum. The *rinzu* has been yūzen dyed to create an all-over pattern of large mandarin orange trees, *tachibana*, and cypress fans, *hiōgi*, on which are scenes from *The Tale of Genji*.

CAT. NO. 20

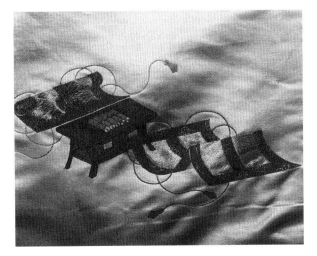

CAT. NO. 24

22. *Furisode*, Late Edo period, nineteenth century. Pl. 25, fig. 8.

Silk, 4/1 satin damask weave, *rinzu*; *ōbōshi shibori* and embroidered with silk and gold-leaf-paper-strip-wrapped silk, in satin stitches; couching. Lined in red silk, plain weave; dyed with *beni*, safflower.

182.8 x 127.7 cm; 72 x 50¼ in.

Gift of Gaylord Donnelley in memory of Frances Gaylord Smith, 1991.636

The *rinzu* patterned with parallel trunks of bamboo trees and leaves has been resist-dyed in a cloudlike pattern and embroidered with pairs of *aoi*, asarum, leaves.

23. *Furisode*, Late Edo period, nineteenth century. Pl. 26, fig. 9.

Silk, 4/1 satin damask weave, *rinzu*; embroidered with silk and gold-leaf-paper-wrapped silk, in satin stitches; laid work, couching, and padded couching. Lined in red silk, plain weave; dyed with *beni*, safflower.

183.8 x 128.8 cm; 72¼ x 50¾ in.

Gift of Gaylord Donnelley in memory of Frances Gaylord Smith, 1991.637

The *rinzu* is patterned with a *sayagata* fret of swastikas over which is scattered a motif of either an individual orchid or a chrysanthemum. Embroidered blossoming plum trees extend from the hem to the shoulder.

24. *Aigi*, Late Edo period, eighteenth century. Pl. 27.

Silk, 4/1 satin damask weave, *rinzu*; tie-dyed. Lined in red silk *chirimen*, crepe; dyed with *beni*, safflower.

185 x 122 cm; 72¾ x 48 in.

Oriental Department Sundry Trust, 1940.1101

The *rinzu* patterned with a *sayagata* fret of swastikas over which is scattered a motif of an individual orchid or a chrysanthemum, is tie-dyed in *kanoko*, "fawn spot" *shibori*, with horizontal rows of a stylized design of flowing water called *Kanze mizu*. Scattered over the water is the tea-plant fruit crest, *cha-nomi mon*.

25. *Kosode*, Late Edo period, late eighteenth century. Pl. 29.

Silk and gold-leaf-paper strips, warp-float faced 2/1 twill weave with twill interlacings of secondary binding warps and supplementary patterning wefts. No lining. An interlining of natural plain weave. This *kosode* would have been for winter use.

164 x 133.7 cm; 64½ x 52⅝ in.

Gift of Mrs. Martin A. Ryerson through the Antiquarian Society of The Art Institute of Chicago, 1897.232

The pattern of alternating rows of a large fanciful fruit cluster and a very stylized flower with leaves appears to be related to the patterning of the Western bizarre-type silks, which were being woven in the early eighteenth century.

26. *Kosode*, Late Edo period, late eighteenth century. Pl. 30, fig. 10.

Silk and gold-leaf-paper-strip-wrapped cotton, warp-float faced 4/1 satin weave with supplementary patterning wefts. Lined with red silk *chirimen*, crepe; dyed with *beni*, safflower. There is an interlining of lightly wadded *mawata*, floss. This padded *kosode* would have been for winter use.

180.5 x 125.8 cm; 71 x 49½ in.

Gift of Mrs. Robert D. Graff, 1957.154

This design of an all-over woven pattern of rows of dragons chasing the sacred jewel amidst stylized clouds is based on a similar Chinese design.

27. *Furisode*, Late Edo period, eighteenth century. Pl. 28.

Silk and gold-leaf-paper strips, plain weave with plain interlacings of secondary binding warps and supplementary patterning wefts, which float in raised patterning. Lined with red silk *chirimen*, crepe; dyed with *beni*, safflower. This padded *furisode* would have been for winter use.

192.9 x 124.9 cm; 76 x 49⅛ in.

Gift of Professor S. Choyo through the Antiquarian Society of The Art Institute of Chicago, 1894.1098

Blossoming plum trees extend from hem to shoulder in opposed vertical serpentine lines, *tatewaku*.

Haori:

28. *Haori*, Taisho period, early twentieth century. Pl. 31.

Silk, plain weave; resist dyed. Lined from shoulder to waist with silk, warp-float-faced 4/1 satin weave with supplementary patterning wefts. The remaining lining is a continuation of the plain weave fabric.

115.8 x 151.9 cm; 45⅝ x 59⅞ in.

Bequest of Mrs. Herman J. Hall, 1933.918a

The patterning of the pink silk lining of clematis, *tessen*, and tendrils would indicate that this is a woman's *haori*. The crest, *mon*, is a plum blossom. The *mon* were covered with a paste resist prior to the dyeing of the garment.

29. *Haori*, Showa period, second quarter of the twentieth century. Pl. 32.

Silk, plain weave double cloth. Lined from the shoulders to the hip line with silk, plain weave patterned in wide horizontal stripes. The remaining lining is a continuation of the double cloth. The patterning would indicate that this is a man's *haori*.

117.2 x 130.3 cm; 46¼ x 51¼ in.

Gift of Mrs. L. J. Drake, 1945.294

The double cloth has a wavy *kasuri*-like pattern and a lattice pattern, *mijin-gōshi*, a plaid.

PLATE I. *Nuihaku* (Nō costume), Momoyama period, sixteenth century (cat. no. I).

PLATE 2. *Nuihaku* (detail of pl. 1).

PLATE 3. *Nuihaku* (detail of pl. 1).

PLATE 4. *Nuihaku* (Nō costume), Middle Edo period, eighteenth century (cat. no. 2).

PLATE 5. *Nuihaku* (Nō costume), Late Edo period, early nineteenth century (cat. no. 3).

PLATE 6. *Surihaku* (Nō costume), Late Edo period, late eighteenth–early nineteenth century (cat. no. 4).

PLATE 7. *Karaori* (Nō costume), Middle to Late Edo period, eighteenth century (cat. no. 5).

PLATE 8. *Karaori* (Nō costume), Late Edo period, late eighteenth–early nineteenth century (cat. no. 6).

PLATE 9. *Atsuita karaori* (Nō costume), Late Edo period, late eighteenth century (cat. no. 7).

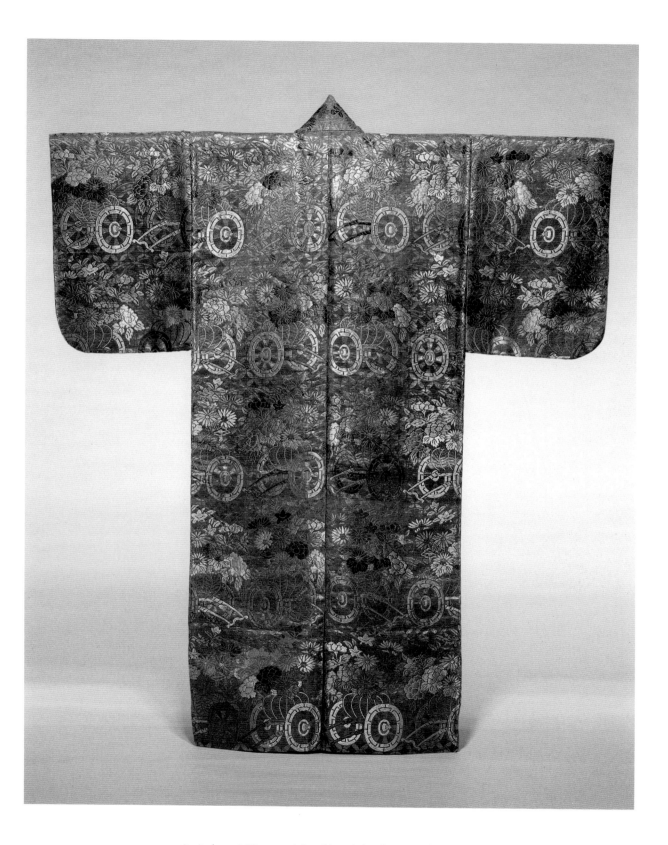

PLATE 10. *Atsuita karaori* (Nō costume), Late Edo period, early nineteenth century (cat. no. 8).

PLATE II. *Atsuita karaori* (Nō costume), Late Edo period, early nineteenth century (cat. no. 9).

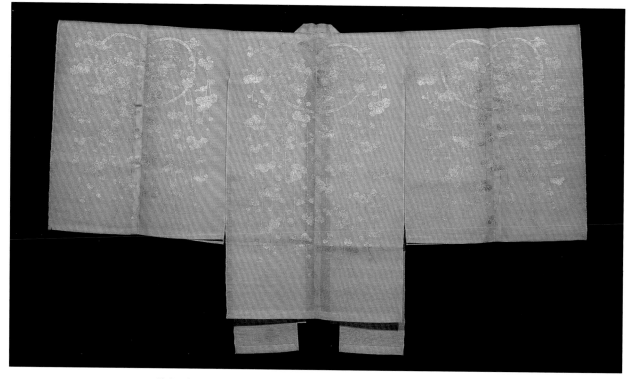

PLATE 12. *Chōken* (Nō costume), Late Meiji–Early Taisho period, early twentieth century (cat. no. 10).

PLATE 13. Unusual *ōsodemono*-style garment, Late Edo period, early nineteenth century (cat. no. 12).

PLATE 14. *Chōken* (Nō costume), Late Edo period, mid-nineteenth century (cat. no. 11).

PLATE 15. Unusual *ōsodemono*-style garment, Meiji period, late nineteenth century (cat. no. 13).

PLATE 16. *Hangiri* (Nō costume), Late Edo period, early nineteenth century (cat. no. 14).

PLATE 17. *Hangiri* (Nō costume), Meiji period, late nineteenth century (cat. no. 15).

PLATE 18. *Awase kariginu* (Nō costume), Late Edo–Early Meiji period, nineteenth century (cat. no. 16).

PLATE 19. *Sashinuki* (Nō costume), Late Edo–Early Meiji period,
nineteenth century (cat. no. 17).

PLATE 20. *Koshi obi* (Nō costume), Late Meiji period, late nineteenth
or early twentieth century (cat. no. 18).

PLATE 21. *Kamishimo* (Kyōgen costume) (trousers), Showa period, first half of twentieth century (cat. no. 19).

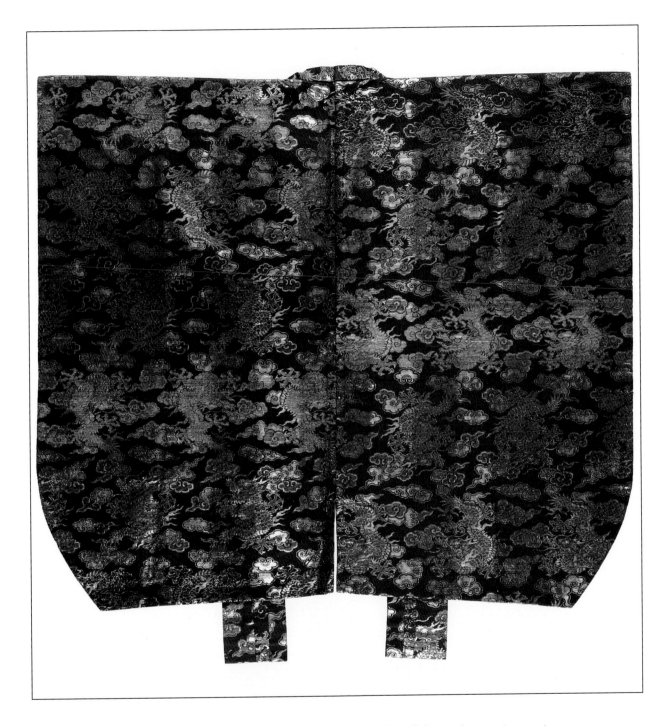

PLATE 22. *Kamishimo* (Kyōgen costume) (jacket), Showa period, first half of twentieth century (cat. no. 19).

PLATE 23. *Uchikake*, Late Edo–Early Meiji period, nineteenth century (cat. no. 20).

PLATE 24. *Furisode*, Late Edo period, nineteenth century (cat. no. 21).

PLATE 25. *Furisode*, Late Edo period, nineteenth century (cat. no. 22).

PLATE 26. *Furisode*, Late Edo period, nineteenth century (cat. no. 23).

PLATE 27. *Aigi*, Late Edo period, eighteenth century (cat. no. 24).

PLATE 28. *Furisode*, Late Edo period, eighteenth century (cat. no. 27).

PLATE 29. *Kosode*, Late Edo period, late eighteenth century (cat. no. 25).

PLATE 30. *Kosode*, Late Edo period, late eighteenth century (cat. no. 26).

PLATE 31. *Haori*, Taisho period, early twentieth century (cat. no. 28).

PLATE 32. *Haori*, Showa period, second quarter of twentieth century (cat. no. 29).

PLATE 33. Kitagawa Utamaro (Japanese, 1753–1806). *Joshoku kaiko tewaza gusa* (*Women's Work in Silk Culture*) (sheet 2), c. 1802.

PLATE 34. Kitagawa Utamaro. *Joshoku kaiko tewaza gusa* (*Women's Work in Silk Culture*) (sheet 10), c. 1802.

Utamaro's Views of Sericulture

JAMES T. ULAK

Associate Curator of Japanese Art
The Art Institute of Chicago

For the Western eye, Utamaro's elegantly conceived female forms, perhaps together with certain of Hokusai's landscapes, have long been representative of the quintessence of Japanese art. The preeminence of the woodblock-print format and of its particular images reflects the sheer quantitative dominance and accessibility of prints in Europe and America from the mid-nineteenth century to the present. Japanese prints satisfied a variety of tastes for beauty, for exotica, and for ethnographic information about a thoroughly mysterious culture.

Familiarity may lull the viewer of Utamaro's series of twelve prints that portray the sericulture process into overlooking the bizarre juxtaposition of traditions in these images. The perfectly coiffured and costumed beauties, offering occasionally suggestive revelations of flesh, are an unlikely group to be undertaking the tedious and exacting work of producing silk. Utamaro, of course, presented in this series yet another variation of his most successful convention, an intimate and voyeuristic look at prostitutes as idealized feminine beauties engaged in quaint or domestic tasks.[1]

Utamaro's principal subject matter—the interdependent worlds of theater and brothel—is representative of the thematic preoccupation of most seventeenth- and eighteenth-century Japanese print artists. With the altogether droll placement of beauties in this intriguing and technologically complex series of vignettes, the artist relied upon the contemporaneous viewer's knowledge of a long tradition of visual representation of trades and crafts. In addition, he catered to an insatiably curious audience that had been touched (albeit through a circuitous route) by the European encyclopedist tradition and

its systematic cataloguing of knowledge. From the early seventeenth century, the advent of substantive contacts with Europe and comparatively low-cost printing processes led to the publication of Japanese illustrated encyclopedias as well as more specific reference material on botany, zoology, mechanical science, and other fields, all of which found a receptive public.

The process of sericulture was exported to Japan from the continent at some time between 200 B.C. and A.D. 200. These dates coincide with the appearance of Han dynasty (206 B.C.–A.D. 200) silk, which reached a world market that extended to the Mediterranean. The high quality and mass production of this silk was possible because of the technological advances made during the preceding three thousand years. Archaeological evidence in Japan includes a saw-toothed wooden implement that was likely an *osa* or yarn guide for a loom. The *Wei chih wo jen chuan* or Wei Chronicle, a third-century Chinese history, in a subsection entitled *Tung-i chuan*, or "Eastern Barbarian Accounts," offers information on the "woren" or "wojen" (the Chinese appellation for the inhabitants of Japan) and remarks on the existence of sericulture in Japan. The first Japanese mention or description of the process is found in the *Nihon Shoki* or *Nihongi*, the thirty-volume official history of Japan compiled in the eighth century. This account notes both government support of the industry and remarks that a tax was levied on silk in Japan from as early as the fifth century.[2]

PLATE 35. Kitagawa Utamaro. *Joshoku kaiko tewaza gusa* (*Women's Work in Silk Culture*) (sheet 9), c. 1802.

The depiction of people engaged in trade or craft is found in a rather early stage in the Japanese painting tradition. The narrative scroll genre, with examples dating from the twelfth century, served both Buddhist and court patrons as a format for recording the biographies of outstanding religious personalities, temple foundings, illustration of literature, and even military campaigns. In addition to the primary narrative provided in a horizontal flow of alternating units of text and image, a wealth of secondary information about daily life in medieval Japan can be culled from background images. For example, in the *Ishiyama-dera engi emaki* (*Legends of Ishiyama Temple*) (c. 1325), scenes of a temple construction depict in great detail many aspects of carpentry as practiced in fourteenth-century Japan.[3] A biography of the monk Kakunyo (1270–1351), third abbot of Honganji (*Boki e*), also from the fourteenth century, contains marvelous descriptions of food preparation in a large Buddhist monastery.[4] There are numerous examples in dozens of other scrolls.

While the sericulture process was not depicted in these early scrolls, the thirteenth-century *Taima mandala engi* (*Origin and History of the Taima Mandala*) contains perhaps the earliest Japanese painted image of a loom.[5] In the eighth century, a large silk tapestry depicting the Amida Buddha presiding over the Western paradise was transported from T'ang China to Japan. This mandala has been a central icon of the Pure Land (Jodo shu) Buddhist sect. With the dramatic rise of Pure Land's popularity in the thirteenth century, this tale of the miraculous origins of the Taima image was, naturally, recounted in a narrative painting format for both proselytizing and aggrandizing purposes. Noteworthy is the prominence accorded to the depiction of the actual process of creating fabric on a loom—it is not an ancillary or background image. Also important are the implicit relationships established between the miraculously salvific and the creative action of weaving.

Yet another tradition of depicting trade and craft emerged as a subcategory of the narrative format. Poetry contests, or *uta awase*, the aristocratic practice of creating and linking verse on suggested themes, were recorded in horizontal scroll paintings with idealized portraits of poets placed adjacent to calligraphed quotations of their verse entries. In the fourteenth century, variations of this format were introduced in which comic and unexpected participants were substituted for the conservative court figures. *Shokunin uta awase*, an imaginary linked-verse exchange between artisans and tradespeople, gave a forum to amusing court satire and allowed the aristocrats some visual record of commoners not usually encountered in daily life. The various stages of sericulture are not referred to in these lighthearted rounds. But the *shokunin*

uta awase pioneered a format in which the odd juxtapositions of high artistic purpose and voyeuristic interest or curiosity could be successfully combined. Parody and substantive information resided comfortably together.[6]

The cataclysmic social change that destabilized Japan for much of the fifteenth and sixteenth centuries ended with the establishment of a centralized government in the early seventeenth century. A new social order placed the merchant class and townsmen at the center of economic power. With this reordering, the iconography of trade and craft achieved a new level of descriptive dignity. Even in the sixteenth century, the *shokunin uta awase*, whatever the humor of written wordplay found in the scrolls, began to incorporate rather straightforward observations of the artisan's image, avoiding the comic representations found in early centuries.

From the early seventeenth century, a new genre of painting celebrated, with panoramic cityscapes, a freshly resurrected Kyoto (*Rakuchu rakugai zu*) and later offered similarly vibrant and optimistic visions of Edo. In these paintings, shop-lined streets hold every kind of merchandise. Where compositional space allows, certain aspects of the manufacture of products can be observed with a glimpse into the shop interiors. Again, the complex process of sericulture is usually represented only in its final stages of weaving or selling bolts of fabric.[7]

The revival of a stabilizing commercial life after several centuries of civil strife also allowed for a regeneration of the silk industry. This opportunity came, however, precisely at the moment when European traders had established a foothold in the western Japanese port of Nagasaki. The Chinese of the Ming Dynasty (1368–1644) enforced a ban on direct trade with Japan, but traders, principally those from Portugal, proved to be efficient go-betweens. Chinese silk, perceived to be of much higher quality than domestic silk, was sought by the Japanese. Silver from Japanese mines was traded to China. The Japanese domestic silk market was handicapped by this trade relationship, with various modifications enforced, until the desire for Chinese silk had to be balanced against the larger political threat posed by the Portuguese and Spanish presence. The isolationist policies enacted by the government during the 1630s brought stringent controls on Japan's contact with the outside world, but stimulated domestic silk production. In addition to the traditional centers of production in western and central Japan, new centers grew up in the east to serve the population of Edo.

The expansion of production surely stimulated interest and curiosity in the silk-making process. As noted above, while general traditions of visual representation of trade and craft were well established (including a multileveled potential for satire), the imaging of

FIGURE 1. Suzuki Harunobu (Japanese, 1724–1770). *Throwing the Shuttle*, 1765. Woodblock print; 27.6 x 20.6 cm. The Art Institute of Chicago, Clarence Buckingham Collection of Japanese Prints (1937.21). Harunobu was the first artist to take full advantage of techniques for polychrome printing. This print may well have been among the first of the multicolored images produced solely from blocks. The woman at the loom is typical of the delicate and refined figures synonymous with Harunobu. It is unclear whether this image was part of a series.

specific and detailed steps of silk production from egg-hatching to weaving would emerge from a reliance on recently imported Chinese models. The first recorded painting on the specific subject of agriculture and sericulture has been attributed to the artist Lou Chu (1090–1162). Records indicate that this painting was executed based on observations of the production of silk around the Hangchou area. The depiciton of "agriculture" was divided into twenty-one stages, and the process of "sericulture" into twenty-four steps. A handscroll painting describing the sericulture process is attributed to the thirteenth-century Chinese painter Liang K'ai. There is reason to believe that this painting reached Japan in the fourteenth or fifteenth century.[8] Copies of this scroll were possibly infuential in the production of a type of seventeenth- and eighteenth-century screen painting that featured scenes of the agricultural processes in the con-text of the four seasons.

It seems, however, most likely that Japanese books and prints that depicted the details of sericulture were based on Chinese books and prints produced at various points in the mid and late Ming Dynasty. For example, in 1676, Kano Eino (1631–1697) adapted Chinese prints made during the T'ien-shun period (1457–1464) to a Japanese idiom. Later, as the format developed, various indigenous details were incorporated. There are examples of prints and manuals produced throughout the eighteenth and nineteenth centuries. Their content in no way attained a level of precision that would have been helpful to technicians. It should be noted that regional variations in aspects of the mechanical process, such as loom types, can be discerned in these generalized descriptions.[9]

The Japanese handbook *Yosan Hiroku* ("Secret Record" of Sericulture), published in 1803, offers a

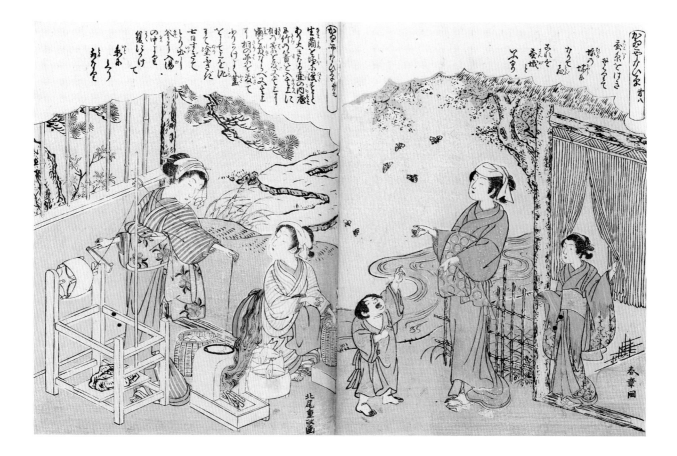

FIGURE 2. Katsukawa Shunshō (Japanese, 1726–1792) and Kitao Shigemasa (Japanese, 1739–1820). *Sanyo Zue, E-hon Takara no itosuji (Treasures of the Thread)* (published by Maekawa Rokuzaemon in 1786), pls. 6–7. 28.5 x 20.5 cm. The Art Institute of Chicago, Ryerson Collection. The images in this book are a joint production of Shunshō and Shigemasa. Shunshō was the leading producer of actor prints in the last quarter of the eighteenth century. Shigemasa, a somewhat less well-known artist, collaborated with Shunshō on a series entitled *Seiro Bijin Awase Sugata Kagami (Mirror of Beautiful Women of the Green Houses)* in 1776. While Shunshō's images of women are decidedly more modest and quaint than those of Utamaro, they are similar enough to suggest that they may have influenced Utamaro's sericulture series, or at least that there may have been a common source for both artists. The "Shigemasa"-signed image on the right is nearly indistinguishable from Shunshō's hand.

FIGURE 3. Katsukawa Shunshō and Kitao Shigemasa. *Sanyo Zue, E-hon Takara no itosuji (Treasures of the Thread)* (published by Maekawa Rokuzaemon in 1786), pl. 12. 28.5 x 20.5 cm. The Art Institute of Chicago, Ryerson Collection. The plate shown here, which is the twelfth and final image in the book, differs both in content and style from Utamaro's later publication (see figs. 4–7). This portrayal of a textile salesman with bolts of fabric and a pattern book is a pragmatic gesture in keeping with the rather quaint, instructive nature of the book.

straightforward and instructive view of the process. This book was a virtual contemporary of the Utamaro series. The book's title underscores the inherent sense of wonder or mystery associated with silk-making.[10]

The Japanese print artist of the eighteenth century catered to an audience eager for views of the several very specific and circumscribed worlds. With some exceptions, the renowned eighteenth-century master designers from Kaigestudō Ando to Suzuki Harunobu—Katsukawa Shunshō, Torii Kiyonaga, and Kitagawa Utamaro—were best known either for their depictions of feminine beauty or theater personalities. It was not until the nineteenth century that the landscape or travel theme established itself. The women who populated the prints were, by and large, demimondain—beauties who serviced the pleasure quarters of the capital.

Utamaro's artistic development was unhurried and was touched by several disparate influences before maturing in the later 1780s. During the 1770s, Utamaro was involved in undistinguished productions, mainly illustrating play guides and librettos for patrons of Kabuki. He also provided images for *kibyoshi* (literally, "yellow cover books"), cheaply produced adult entertainment featuring comedy and social satire. In the late

かいこやしなひ草 十一

枝綿汁のそびめは
いづまーとふーとと
かく孫とも衣
ニてま唐の
んりやも
の大臭しや
帝九汁と心
うらや
よくて又礼記
のうらう汁
ー天り我
中細て綿ん
ち又巳き祥
大巳毛祥
右子伝婦
色もふ時父
世きたんと
須秋とて汁
をいて祢の
經老ふに綵て
ぶりものしよ
死りもとし
三徒山よる
のり

勝川春章画

FIGURE 4 a,b,c. Kitagawa Utamaro (Japanese, 1753–1806). *Joshoku kaiko tewaza gusa* (*Women's Work in Silk Culture*), c. 1802. Woodblock prints; 38.1 x 25.4 cm each. The Art Institute of Chicago, Clarence Buckingham Collection of Japanese Prints (1925.3246–48) (sheets 1–3). See also pl. 33. These prints, which must be read from right to left, depict the first stages of the silk-making process. On the right, the women are portrayed brushing silkworm eggs from the papers upon which they were laid and putting them into hatching boxes. In the middle print, the women gather mulberry leaves to feed caterpillars. The print on the left depicts the process of chopping mulberry leaves and feeding the pieces to the young caterpillars, a process that was repeated five times daily.

1770s, Utamaro produced some actor prints after the style of Katsukawa Shunshō (1726–1792), arguably the day's dominant artist of that genre. Gradually, during the decade of the 1780s, Utamaro sensed his metier and developed a style initially quite dependent, in composition and figural representaton, on the work of Torii Kiyonaga (1752–1815). Kiyonaga rendered female figures that were slightly attenuated but, generally, anatomically convincing. They were often anchored in the foreground of believable and recognizable space. Kiyonaga's diptychs and triptychs provided the appropriate sweep of horizontal perspective for his views of Edo landscape.[11]

Utamaro was entranced with the female form and paid homage with keen observation of the relationships between physical deportment and psychological revelation. He developed the Kiyonaga formula featuring groups of interacting females. These women were, like Kiyonaga's, often placed in gardens, bustling streets, or on riverbanks. But others were comported in space defined not by landscape but rather by the skillful placement of figures in relationship to various objects of domesticity: hanging or strewn garments, laundry, bedding or the bath. Bodies and objects suggest, by their placement, some angles of recession and depth of space. These compositions, however, are usually played out against a monochromatic background. Relationships are presented like jewels on a cloth, visually secured and unchallenged by competing views. Utamaro's productions of the 1790s heightened the focus on the individual form. His masterful bust portraits have become the most recognizable and distinctive of his creations. While perhaps not portraits in the most precise sense, Utamaro depicted a range of emotions, partly observed and partly a clichéd imposition of what might be a stock range of expected female moods. These visages moved well beyond generic presentations of form and infused an individuality that was not previously present in renderings of women.[12]

The publication of Utamaro's series of sericulture prints, *Joshoku kaiko tewaza gusa*, is dated to approximately 1802. Within two years of the appearance of this series, Utamaro was embroiled in a controversy that would lead to his imprisonment. He incensed government officials with what was perceived as an unflattering or satirical portrayal of Toyotomi Hideyoshi (1537–1598), revered military leader and national unifier. A rather brief incarceration initiated a period of decline from which the artist did not recover. He died in 1806 at the age of fifty-four. Utamaro's decline because of an alleged political slight seems a curious fate for an artist whose genius was almost wholly focused on idealized representations of the feminine. Some would suggest that the death of his friend and advisor, the publisher Tsutaya

Jūzaboro (1750–1797), left Utamaro bereft of encouragement and guidance at a critical point in his development. While the cause of Utamaro's fall remains mysterious, there is general agreement today that the quality of his work declined during the early years of the nineteenth century. He can be seen reverting to formulas successful a decade or more earlier.

The sericulture series seems to respond to a sustained audience interest in the actual silk making process. Various artists active in the latter half of the eighteenth century manipulated the formulaic presentation.[13] Particularly instructive for an appreciation of Utamaro's version is the print series created by Shunshō in 1772 (see fig. 1)[14] and a book published in 1786 featuring images of the sericulture process with alternating plates designed by Shunshō and Kitao Shigemasa (1739–1820) (see figs. 2–3).[15] Both the print series and the book clarify the extent to which the presentation of the sericulture process relied on a rather stock formula. It seems highly likely that Utamaro knew of and used the Shunshō and/or the Shunshō and Shigemasa versions. The 1786 book lacks the attention given to single-pulled prints; the quality of impression and paper was obviously less important than the mass production and dissemination of a popular item.

The composition of Utamaro's *Joshoku kaiko tewaza gusa* seems to be structured as a series of four triptychs.[16] The prints are numbered from one through twelve, and they are best understood as a unified composition if read in the Japanese fashion, from right to left.[17] With the exception of the final sheet, a brief explanation of the stages of the process is printed in the scalloped cloud convention at the top of each print. The final sheet does not go unexplained; rather, the written matter on the eleventh sheet (fig. 7b) includes an explanation of the twelfth sheet (fig. 7a).

In the first sheet (fig. 4c), two women brush silkworm eggs into a hatching box with a feather, while another woman looks on. The flowering tree at the right of the scene suggests the spring and surely the month of March, when this step of the process was initiated. The second image (fig. 4b and pl. 33) portrays three women harvesting mulberry leaves, the staple for silkworms. The scalloped cloud joins the first two sheets. At the left of the second sheet a vertical post signals a movement toward an element on the third sheet (fig. 4a) and toward the scene of hatching trays on open framed shelves. In the foreground, women prepare finely chopped mulberry leaves to be spread on the trays to nourish the hatched worms.

The rack structure flows into the fourth sheet (fig. 5c) where women are seen brushing away dried mulberry leaves and transferring the well-nourished worms to another set of trays. The worms are given a resting, or "sleeping" period. The fifth scene (fig. 5b) shows women

FIGURE 5 a,b,c. Kitagawa Utamaro. *Joshoku kaiko tewaza gusa* (*Women's Work in Silk Culture*), c. 1802. Woodblock prints; 38.1 x 25.4 cm each. The Art Institute of Chicago, Clarence Buckingham Collection of Japanese Prints (1925.3249–51) (sheets 4–6). The print on the right depicts the removing of dried pieces of mulberry leaves from the feeding trays with a feather, and the placing of the trays upon racks where they are kept at an even temperature while the caterpillars are dormant. In the middle print, women feed the nearly full-grown caterpillars with whole mulberry leaves. In the final print of this triptych, the women are seen examining the newly-spun cocoons.

attending what is called "the great awakening." The large and rested silkworms awake with ravenous appetites and women shower them with fresh, whole mulberry leaves. In the sixth stage of the sequence (fig. 5a), worms with fully spun cocoons are arranged on trays and again racked.

The seventh and eighth scenes (figs. 6b–c) refer to the regenerative stages when moths emerge from the cocoons, lay eggs, and depart. In the seventh scene, women use threads to coax moths to deposit their eggs on a paper. Once that essential process is complete, the moths are observed, in the eighth scene, flying off for the brief remainder of their life cycle. The ninth scene (fig. 6a and pl. 35) depicts the shed cocoons being boiled and the silk thread being reeled onto a hand-turned spindle.

The tenth sheet (fig. 7c and pl. 34) shows the outer winding of the cocoon being pulled on posts into *mawata*, or floss silk, while silk is also hung on lines. In the unified image of the eleventh and twelfth sheets (figs. 7a–b), silk is spun and woven on a loom. Explanations in the cloud shapes offer this rather basic procedural information. In the eleventh sheet, however, the inscription continues with the notation that the gods Kagutsuchi and Haniyama hime gave birth to Wakamusubi. A silk worm and mulberry tree grew on the head of Wakamusubi. The inscription further states that sericulture was introduced in Japan by the wife of Emperor Yuryaku and was started in China during the reign of the Emperor Huang Ti. This "historical" afternote posits a fifth-century arrival of sericulture in Japan. As explained above, the evidence suggests a somewhat earlier arrival.

In addition to the numbering, series title, and explanatory inscriptions, each sheet contains the printed seal of the publisher, Tsuruya Kieimon, and a printed signature reading *Utamaro fude*, "by the brush of Utamaro."

Several editions of this series are known. The edition in the collection of The Art Institute of Chicago, which is reproduced here, is understood to be the earliest, with a distinctive color scheme of green, yellow, pale gray, violet, and blue. A second edition included red. It should be noted that an edition that is generally agreed to be a late-nineteenth- or early-twentieth-century edition has no explanatory text in the scalloped clouds.

Utamaro moves the viewer through the twelve-print series with a quite traditional convention of diagonal thrusts. This is the technique most frequently employed in the horizontal narrative scroll. Most scenes use some type of triangular grouping of women. The paraphernalia of silk production, while rendered in comparatively abbreviated form, occupy much of the composition. Wherever possible, the artist makes the most of contrasting structural linearity and rounded forms. Still, the

FIGURE 6 a,b,c. Kitagawa Utamaro. *Joshoku kaiko tewaza gusa* (*Women's Work in Silk Culture*), c. 1802. Woodblock prints; 38.1 x 25.4 cm each. The Art Institute of Chicago, Clarence Buckingham Collection of Japanese Prints (1925.3252–54) (sheets 7–9). See also pl. 35. In the print on the right, the women are portrayed as guiding the moths with a thread so that they will lay their eggs on sheets of paper. As we move from right to left, we find the women in the middle print watching the moths fly away after they have laid their eggs. The print on the left depicts the women boiling the cocoons and reeling off the filament of silk.

expansive elegance of some of Utamaro's earlier multi-figure creations is missing from this series. Perhaps one of the most visually effective of the twelve prints is the final one depicting weaving at a loom. The immediate background and far distance are left clear, effectively framing Utamaro's characteristically refined shapes.

Comparisons with the Shunshō/Shigemasa book (1786), as noted earlier, suggest an obvious source employed by Utamaro. Several other features are noteworthy. The final page of the book contains an image not found in the Utamaro series. A merchant is depicted presenting bolts of silk for selection by clients. This is a logical, if rather prosaic and literal, conclusion to the sequence. It is, however, in keeping with the cheerfully didactic mood of the preceding images. Female forms, as rendered by Shunshō and Shigemasa, are charming, diminutive, and fully integrated into the intention of the prints. Utamaro offers the viewer/reader a comparable body of information, but at every point suggestive beauty invites the eye to linger on more than worms and leaves. The Utamaro women seem to exude an air of determined amateurism, their attire not quite appropriate to the task. In the final sheet of the sequence, the woman at the loom, with strands of hair falling across her face and kimono opened to expose her breast, is an Utamaro cliché which best expresses the purpose of the series.

The various printed representations of silk production found in Japanese art of the eighteenth and nineteenth centuries are ample evidence of the curiosity stimulated by a mysterious, yet economically vital, process. The Utamaro series, whatever its ultimate value in relation to the artist's oeuvre, stands beyond the didactic. It is one of the final entries in a long Japanese tradition of offering playful views of the commonplace. The stately court poetry competitions of the thirteenth century served as the visual and intellectual foil for beggars, iron-mongers, and carpenters. In the rapidly changing world of eighteenth-century Japan, the pretensions of religion and politics, and the tedium of daily work, were imaginatively immersed and mixed with the women of Edo's demimonde. The result was a delightful combination of information, humor, and satire.

FIGURE 7 a,b,c. Kitagawa Utamaro. *Joshoku kaiko tewaza gusa* (*Women's Work in Silk Culture*), c. 1802. Woodblock prints; 38.1 x 25.4 cm each. The Art Institute of Chicago, Clarence Buckingham Collection of Japanese Prints (1925.3255–57) (sheets 10–12). See also pl. 34. In this final triptych, Utamaro portrays the final stages of silk-making. Reading the prints from right to left, the first depicts women drying the coarse outer winding from the cocoons and making it into sheets of *mawata*, or floss silk; the second shows the grading and spinning of the silk; and the third finds the women weaving cloth from the silk.

Hinagata Bon:
The Art Institute of Chicago
Collection of Kimono Pattern Books

BETTY Y. SIFFERT

The Art Institute of Chicago

The Asian Art Department and Ryerson Library collections of Japanese picture books (*e-hon*) at The Art Institute of Chicago began at the end of the last century with a gift from Martin A. Ryerson, founder of the museum's library and one of the Art Institute's earliest and greatest benefactors. Ryerson's gift was drawn from his own collection of books.

Under the guidance of Frederick W. Gookin, who was named curator of the Buckingham Collection of woodblock prints in 1914, significant additions were made through purchases from fine collections that came on the market in the early decades of this century. In 1923, the collection was augmented with a large part of the picture-book collection acquired by Ernest Fenollosa, an early curator of the Oriental Department of the Museum of Fine Arts, Boston, during his years of residency in Japan.

In 1931, a descriptive catalogue of both the Japanese and Chinese books in the Art Institute's collections was published.[1] This catalogue remains an important source of information because of its detailed descriptions of the books in the collections. In his introduction to the catalogue, Kenji Toda, the compiler and editor, explained the focus of the core collection of Japanese picture books: a history of Japanese painting in the Edo period (1603–1868) that would supplement the Buckingham Collection of *ukiyo-e* prints, providing insights into the development of the woodblock print and the background of the major *ukiyo-e* artists. *Ukiyo-e* means literally "pictures of the floating (or transient) world," and it refers to a school of artists whose paintings and woodblock prints depicted the world of Edo period Japan.

The collection grew with the acquisition of books of the Meiji era (1868–1912), in part through gifts of works collected by artists who had lived and worked in Japan around the turn of the century. Among these acquisitions was the collection of Louise Norton Brown, which Martin Ryerson purchased and presented to the museum in 1919. This collection is of particular interest here because it provided most of the kimono pattern books of the Meiji era in the museum's collection.[2]

After the death of Frederick Gookin in 1936, a memorial gift from his library of Japanese art books was presented to the museum. This large collection included significant works from both the Edo and Meiji periods.

Generally, *hinagata bon* means "design book" or "pattern book." But in discussing the Japanese *e-hon*, or picture book, the expression is used more specifically to refer to the block-printed books of *kosode* or kimono patterns, the first of which was published in 1666 and was entitled *Shinsen O-Hinagata* (*A New Selection of Respected Patterns*).[3]

Because most of the museum's early *e-hon* were chosen to support the Buckingham Collection of woodblock prints, many *hinagata bon* of the Edo period in the collection are works by major *ukiyo-e* artists. The number of such books by each was small, especially in comparison to their work in *ukiyo-e*, but it was very significant, for kimono designers were held in the highest regard as artists. Some not only designed books of patterns but actually painted garments. Several, such as Hishikawa Moronobu (d. 1694), were members of designer families.[4] Some books in the Art Institute's collection have no identified artist, possibly because of the loss of title pages, but they are important in the study of the culture of the Edo period within which the *ukiyo-e* artists worked. Their presence is evidence that the Art Institute's collection of *hinagata bon* from this period is quite representative.

Hinagata bon were working documents intended for use by the draper in helping his patron select a new garment. Many were produced by drapers or cloth merchants themselves, or at a draper's direction. Most of those that survive show great wear; covers, title pages, and other parts have, in some instances, been lost. This condition is common to many of the older *e-hon*, but is compounded in the case of these heavily used fashion books.

Early *hinagata bon* had a rather standard form: on each page, an outline of the back of a garment was filled in with a proposed pattern or design. The designer might add some instructions concerning color and the process of copying the design; sometimes poetic names were provided, or admonitions were added about how the garment should be worn. This basic format was retained by many designers into the Meiji period. The Art Institute's collection includes other types of books related to textiles and garment design that were also used in kimono making.

The *hinagata bon* from the Meiji period are generally, with a few important exceptions, the work of designers who were unknown in the West then and now. This is understandable because, by the beginning of the twentieth century, the focus of many of the publishers turned to annual volumes reflecting the newest fashions, which would render obsolete the previous year's designs. Louise Norton Brown explained that the older books were "found in all the secondhand book shops of Japan . . .[and were] comparatively inexpensive."[5] She suggested that useful and lovely collections could have been formed of such works, had they only been recognized. The Art Institute has almost one hundred Meiji *hinagata bon*, most of which are from Brown's collection.

In the figure captions that follow, the comments on books dating from the Edo period are based on the descriptive catalogue by Kenji Toda.

FIGURE I. *Onna Shorei Shū* (*Collection of Rules of Etiquette for Women*), Volume I: *Dress and Table Manners*. Published by Yamada Ichirobei (1660 [Manji 3]). 7 volumes, complete. 27 x 17 cm. (Ryerson Library 761.952 M86on)

This was one of many "useful books for women" published in the Edo period and was directed to the bride and young matron. Drawings of *kosode* (forerunners of the present-day kimono), which are portrayed as draped across lacquer racks on several pages in this volume, were guides to current fashion and popular design motifs. While this book predates the first *hinagata bon*, published in 1666, designs such as this could serve the same function; the draper could easily follow the drawing in making a garment selected by his patron.

The illustrations in this book have been attributed to the first *ukiyo-e* artist, Hishikawa Moronobu.

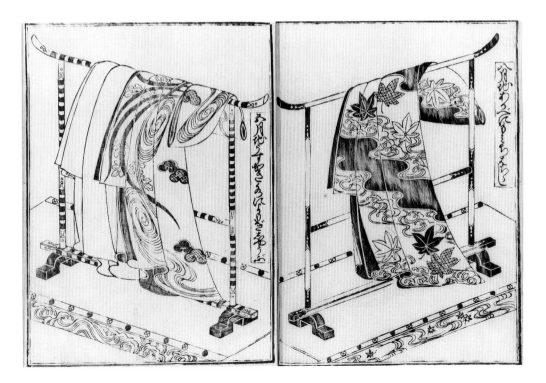

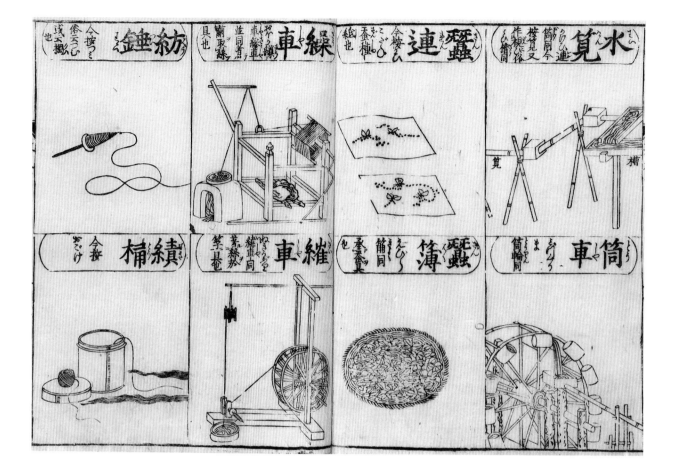

FIGURE 2. *Kunmō Zu-i* (*A Collection of Pictures for Primary Instruction*), Volume 10: *Utensils* (Kyoto, 1669–1695). Nakamura Tekisai, compiler. Eighteen of twenty volumes published by Yamagataya. 27 x 17 cm. (Ryerson Library 761.952 K961k)

The first edition of this work, published in 1660, was the earliest Japanese illustrated encyclopedia.[6] This illustration is largely devoted to aspects of building tools and agriculture. Pictured here are several objects related to sericulture, which was almost exclusively the work of farm women. On the right page, upper left, young silkworms are spread on paper for sorting, with a picture below of cocoons formed by the worms on a tray. On the left page, upper right, is the winding of silk filament from a cocoon in boiling water. (See, in this issue, James T. Ulak, "Utamaro's Views of Sericulture," figs. 4c, 5a, and 6a) Above each picture are the Chinese character and Japanese name for the object, with references, on the left, to other related items.

The Art Institute has eight volumes from the first edition of this work, and ten from the second, which appears to have undergone several permutations between 1669 and 1695.

FIGURE 3. *Kosode No Sugatami* (*The Full-length Mirror of Kosode*) (1682). Hishikawa Moronobu, artist. 23 sheets. 18.5 x 13.5 cm. Formerly Arthur W. Dow Collection.

Moronobu (d. 1694) was both the first major *ukiyo-e* woodblock print artist and one of the period's most prolific illustrators of books.[7] In this small volume there are twenty-three pages of one or two women in decorative *kosode*, each facing a page with a garment design in the *hinagata* format. The book was designed for the draper, who could easily reproduce a garment from the clear delineation of pattern the artist had provided. On some pages, the user is instructed to use *chirimen*, a silk crepe, and is given needlework instructions for both the outside of the garment and its lining.

This work probably had popular appeal as well, since it is characteristic of Moronobu's rendition of the graceful female form in some of the loveliest of early *ukiyo-e*, done at the height of his career.[8]

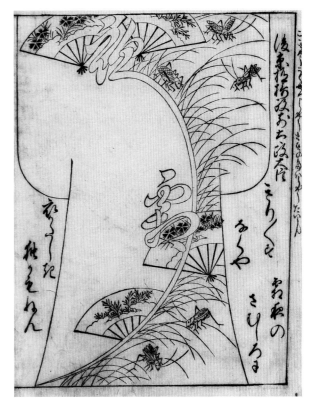

FIGURE 4. *"Kimono Designs"* (Edo [Tokyo]: Yezōshiya Hachiyemon, and Kyoto: Yezōshiya Kisayemon, 1688 [Jōkyō 8]). Title and artist not given. This is the second of a probable two-volume set. 25 sheets. 27 x 19 cm. (Ryerson Library 761.952 K49)

In this work, each *hinagata*-style design is directly related to one of the poems in *Hyakunin-Isshu* ("Verses by One Hundred Poets"), an anthology of classical Japanese poetry dating from the thirteenth century and still very popular in Japan. To the right of each design is the name of the poet, with a five-line poem inscribed on each side of the garment. Each design reflects the artist's reaction to the sentiment of the poem, sometimes with a line or phrase from the poem incorporated into the pattern.

This volume contains the second group of fifty poems in the anthology, suggesting that the first fifty were in volume 1. The work reflects the union of literature, visual art with traditional themes or motifs, and textile decoration, which is characteristic of the history of Japanese art.

These volumes are quite typical of the *hinagata bon* format; the set's worn condition suggests heavy use for its primary purpose—to provide pattern ideas for the patron and the kimono maker.

Pictured is a pattern with a small "checkerboard" design, which could have been executed in a variety of ways depending on the wishes of the patron, the expertise of the kimono artisan, or the intent of the designer. In one of *nuihaku* in the Art Institute's collection (pl. 4; cat. no. 2), the squares of "checkerboard" design were executed in silver leaf impressed on the fabric with a needlework overlay.

Because the volume is incomplete and only four of the 54 sheets present have artists' signatures, the different artists' work cannot be clearly identified, and there may be work in the volume by other artists.

This pattern book is devoted to a single theme long used in many of the visual arts as well as in *kosode* and kimono design: the flowering plum tree and the plum blossom, representative of early spring because it often starts blooming in February. The Art Institute's red silk embroidered *furisode* with plum tree design (pl. 26; cat. no. 23) is a masterful intrepretation of this popular theme that appears in the pattern on the right.

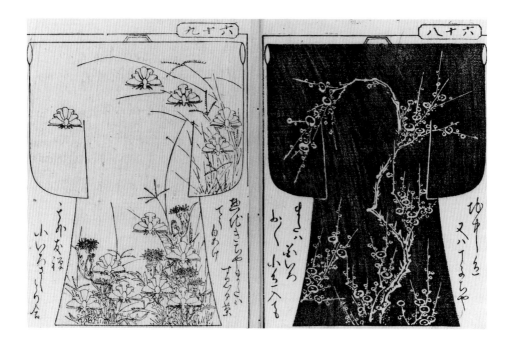

FIGURE 8. *Yehon Sakaegusa* (*Picture Book of a Prosperous Household*) (Edo [Tokyo]: Izumiya Ichibei, 1790 [Kwansei 2]). Katsukawa Shunshō, author of preface. Kastukawa Shunchō, artist; signed: Gōto Gakō Cūrinsha Katsukawa Shunchō. 2 volumes, bound in one, complete. Color. 20.5 x 15 cm. (Ryerson Library 761.952 S562s)

Katsukawa Shunshō (1726–1792) was a leading *ukiyo-e* artist in the late eighteenth century whose greatest works were prints representing actors. These prints are heavily represented in the collection of the Art Institute. Shunshō gave this book its title. Katsukawa Shunchō (fl. 1780–1795) was his pupil, and worked on both prints and book illustrations.

The pages reproduced here are from the first volume, illustrating a young woman's homelife. Represented are preparations for a wedding: selecting fabrics from the finished *tan*, or bolts of silk, and the hand-sewing of the kimono trousseau.

FIGURE 7. *Hinagata Some-Iro No Yama* (*Patterns: The Mountain of Dye Colors*) (Subtitle: *Tōryū Kōrin Shin-Moyō* [*New Patterns in the Modern Style of Kōrin*]) (Kyoto: Kikuya Kihei, 1732 [Kyōhō 17]). Kyoto, Nonomura, artist (probably Nonomura Chūbei). 3 volumes, complete. 26.5 x 18.5 cm. (Ryerson Library 761.952 C559h)

There are 112 patterns in these volumes for women's kimono that are primarily derived from the works of Ogata Kōrin (1658–1716), one of Japan's greatest painters and designers. Each pattern was given a name, generally a flower or plant; the designer also added notes about appropriate colors to be used in the yuzen-dyeing process.

As shown in this book, most designs of the first half of the eighteenth century used the full back of the garment for a design, which generally swept from the right shoulder toward the left hem. The garment was either worn loosely as a cloak over a kimono or was tied with a very narrow sash, the *obi*, so as not to interfere with the pattern.

The kimono pattern on the left uses the flowing plum tree combined with the pictorial fan. A similar theme appears in the Art Institute's *furisode* with mandarin oranges and fans in its design (pls. 24; cat. no. 21).

Katsushika Hokusai (1760–1849) was a preeminent print artist and painter, perhaps Japan's best known.

Komon are small, repeat patterns, at the time especially popular among the samurai class for semiformal and informal kimono. Later in the Edo period, they became generally popular with all classes as the sumptuary laws restricting elaborate dress were increasingly enforced.

In this small book, Hokusai presented many intricate geometric patterns and instructions for the efficient copying of each by the textile artisan. According to the preface, the patterns are Hokusai's original designs. Generally, the resulting drawings would have been transferred to fabric using stencils; the length of fabric would then have been vat-dyed to achieve the desired pattern. This book was to be followed by another related to needlework designs for garments, but this volume was apparently never completed.[9]

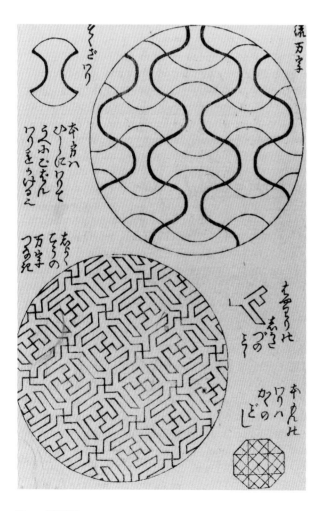

Sukenobu (1671–1751) was a leading illustrator of books during the middle Edo period, producing several *hinagata bon*, as well as an *ukiyo-e* artist. In this volume, instead of using the *hinagata* outline format, he sought greater popular appeal by showing graceful young women modeling his designs. Above each figure, he provided a fanciful *mon*, or crest, along with instructions on how a woman might achieve each of the thirty-two Buddhist ideal graces: nobility, longevity, dignity, etc. On some pages, he also discussed women's ethics and behavior.[10]

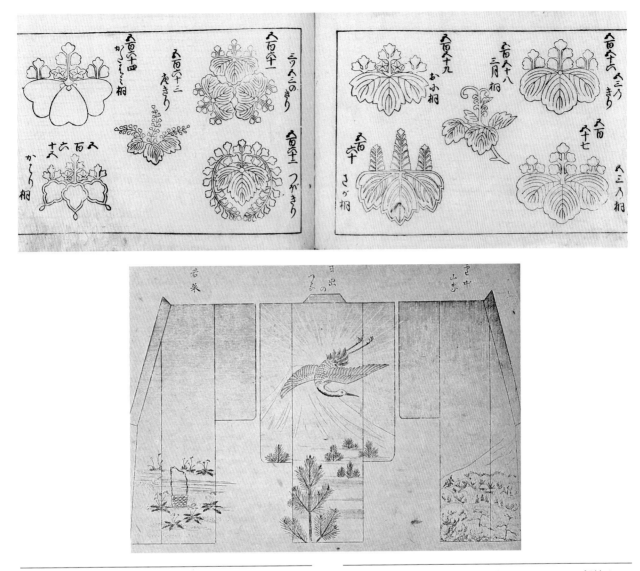

FIGURE 11. *Monchō Zushiki Kōmoku* (*Book of Classified Forms of Crests*) (Osaka: Aburaya Jinshichi, 1762 [Horeki 12]). Taga Kinsuke, artist. Murakami Kōsuke, engraver. 1 volume, complete. Gift of Frederick W. Gookin Memorial Collection. (Ryerson Library 745.44952 T121m)

Most of this book consists of sets of illustrations showing how a basic, traditional motif for a *mon* such as the pine tree, the fan, the paulownia leaf, etc., can be modified to provide a great variety of designs. At the end of the book are several pages of instructions for copying based on the basic geometry of the designs. These instructions could have been used in a variety of visual arts or could have been adapted for practical purposes such as creating merchant signs.

FIGURE 12. *Koyeki Non Chō Taizen: Kodai Moyō* (*Ornaments of Old: A Collection of Designs*) (Kyoto: Nakamura Asako, 1891 [Meiji 24]). Kyūsaburō Kaiyama, designer. 3 volumes, complete. 11 x 16 cm. Gift of Frederick W. Gookin Memorial Collection. (Ryerson Library 745.44952 K13k)

These small volumes provide a wide variety of designs for crests, borders, textiles, and *kanji* characters, in many cases with diagrams for their reproduction in various art forms. Pictured here is a variation on the *hinagata* outline for the kimono. In addition to the back, both left and right fronts are shown in outline with the placement of the design. By the time this book was published, the *obi*, or sash, had reached its present width of 30 centimeters (about 14 inches), with a large decorative tie in the back that had to be considered in the surface design of the garment. Generally, the important elements of the pattern were moved to the bottom of the kimono, to the lower sleeve, and sometimes to the upper back and shoulders.

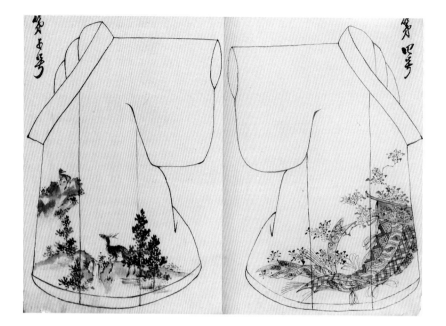

FIGURE 13. *Hinagata Bon*-style work, possibly a sketchbook. Title page information missing; probably produced beteween 1874 and 1901. 1 volume, complete. 26.5 x 19.5 cm. Gift of Martin A. Ryerson, purchased from Louise Norton Brown Collection. (Ryerson Library 745.44952 H653)

Each design shows half of the garment back and one side of the front. All designs were hand drawn and some were enhanced with subtle color. This unknown artist had the lyrical touch of some of the earlier *ukiyo-e* masters. The depiction of a brocade curtain of classical Japanese design could have been strikingly realized in embroidery, much as a similar pattern is in the Art Institute's *uchikake* (pl. 23; cat. no. 20).

FIGURE 14. *Hinagaromo* (*Designs for Kimono: Moon*) (Kyoto: Honda Ichijiro, 1906 [Meiji 39]). Kiyoe Tabata, artist. One volume of probably a larger set. Color. 32.5 x 23 cm. Gift of Martin A. Ryerson, purchased from the Louise Norton Brown Collection. (Ryerson Library 745.44952 T11hi)

Early in the twentieth century, this artist (Kiyoe Tabata) and publisher (Honda Ichijiro) issued several annual sets of kimono designs reflecting the latest in fashions, much as the design houses do today. In this work and others, there was an emphasis on a dark background fabric, using strong colors of brown, purple, green, and, of course, black. These colors remain popular in Japan with married and mature women who still wear kimono for ceremonial occasions.

Patterns with major design elements in the middle, such as that pictured, were probably for *haori* or *uchikake*, which were worn loosely over the *obi*-tied kimono. In the finished garment, the draper would add the wearer's family *mon* where the white circles appear on the shoulders.

Glossary

Prepared by Mary V. Hays and Ralph E. Hays in collaboration with Lorna Ann Filippini and Christa C. Thurman.

As indicated below, some of the terms that follow are defined in the table "Types of Nō Costumes," pp. 26–27.

aigi. A full-length woman's *kosode* worn under an *uchikake*. Usually patterned with *kanoko shibori.*

Ainu. The descendents of Caucasian aboriginal settlers of Japan, originally called Yezo (Ezo), the name of the northern area of Japan now called Hokkaido, to which these people first migrated and where they now live.

Aki no nanakusa. See **The Seven Plants of Autumn.**

aoi. Asarum caulescens Maxim. Also called *futaba aoi* or *kamo aoi.* The English common name for asarum is wild ginger. Frequently *aoi* has been translated incorrectly as "hollyhock," which is *Althaea rosea* of the *Malvaceae* family.

aoi, fuyu. Malva verticillata Linnaeus. A flowering trailing vine with leaves resembling ivy.

aoi, mizu. Monochoria korsakovii Regel et Maack. A flowering plant with heart-shaped leaves that grows near water.

asa no ha. Literally "hemp leaf." A geometric leaf that vaguely resembles a hemp leaf.

atsuita (costume). *See* "Types of Nō Costumes."

atsuita (fabric). The fabric used for the *kosode* worn for the Nō drama roles that require an *atsuita* costume. In the sixteenth century, this was a stiff, heavy, patterned fabric imported from China. Japanese weavers soon began to weave a similar fabric. *Atsuita* is the name of the thick board around which the imported Chinese fabric was wrapped.

atsuita karaori (costume). *See* "Types of Nō Costumes."

atsuita karaori (fabric). The fabric used for the costumes worn for the Nō drama roles that require an *atsuita karaori* costume. It has patterning typical of *atsuita* fabric but these patterns are woven with the long supplementary weft floats used in weaving *karaori.* It was first woven at Nishijin in Kyoto in the second half of the seventeenth century.

awase kariginu. See kariginu.

beni. See benibana.

benibana. A dye extracted from the petals of the thistle, *Carthamus tinctorius L.,* called "safflower" in English. The scarlet color, *beni,* resulting from many dippings fades when exposed to heat such as sunlight.

bizarre silk. The term "bizarre" in textile terminology refers to early eighteenth-century woven silks of French origin. "Bizarre" corresponds to extraordinary patterns that cannot be described in any other way. As a description, the term was first used by Dr. Vilhelm Sloman in the title of a book *Bizarre Designs in Silks,* written in 1953 and published in Copenhagen.

brocading wefts. *See* **wefts, supplementary brocading.**

chigobakama. See "Types of Nō Costumes."

chirimen. A plain weave silk crepe fabric. The warp is untwisted, unglossed thread and the weft is highly twisted, unglossed thread. For the weft, several unglossed threads are either S-twisted or Z-twisted together 1500 to 3500 times. These twisted weft threads are then starched to retain the twist while weaving. Usually in the weaving two shots are made with S-twisted weft followed by two shots with Z-twisted weft. After weaving, the starch and sericin are washed out of the fabric and the twist in the wefts is released, creating a fabric with a crinkled surface.

There are many variations in the weaving of *chirimen.* Each has a specific name.

chōken. See "Types of Nō Costumes."

couching. A needlework technique where threads are laid over a pattern line or area and held in place by short stitches made through a foundation fabric. These couching stitches can be executed in a variety of stitches and patterns.

daimyo. A feudal lord possessing large fiefs or areas of land and occupying the highest position in the warrior class.

dangawari. Literally "levels different." One of the three types of sectional placement of patterning on *kosode,* in which two different horizontal bands of patterning are adjacent to each other across a vertical seam. Originally, these *kosode* were made by sewing together large pieces of different fabrics. Later fabrics were woven that were patterned with alternating horizontal squares.

degummed silk thread. *See* **glossed silk thread.**

dōbuku. A man's outer coat, worn by the upper echelon of the warrior class from the fourteenth to the early seventeenth century. The forerunner of the present day *haori.*

donsu. See **satin damask weave, *donsu.***

double cloth. A weave with two warp sets, each interlacing with its own weft set or sets, put on a loom so that two textiles are woven in layers simultaneously. These cloths can be completely separate from one another, joined by stitching ties, joined at the selvages, or joined through patterning achieved by exchanging the position of each cloth on the loom while weaving.

embroidering. The action of embellishing a foundation fabric with decorative stitches by using needle and thread.

Ezo *nishiki.* *See* *nishiki.*

fan paper or **mount.** These are paintings done within the contours of a fan so that they can be mounted as a fan.

flat gold-paper thread. *See* **gold-paper thread, flat.**

float or **floats.** A warp or weft passing unbound over two or more elements of the opposite set.

floss, silk. Silk thread from which the sericin has been removed so that it is soft and lustrous. The term is used also for tangled waste silk.

fuki. An "addition" or extension at the hemline of a *kosode*, especially the *uchikake*. It is a roll of padding covered by the lining that both weights the garment, thereby controlling the fall of the skirt, and protects the expensive fabric of the *kosode* from soil and wear.

fukusa. An embroidered, dyed, or painted square fabric cover with a lining that is laid over a gift when presented by the giver.

furisode. Literally "swinging or waving sleeves." A long-sleeved variation of the *kosode* worn by children and unmarried women on special occasions.

fusenryō. Literally "floating-line design." Originally a generic term for textile designs woven in relief but later applied to large medallion-like motifs both flat and in relief.

gauze weave. A weave characterized by the interworking or crossing of warps between weft passes. In simple gauze weaves the warps cross and return to their original order on each two successive weft passes and maintain an order of warp interworking and weft interlacing.

Complex gauze weaves have variations in both the order and sequence in which the warps interwork as well as variations in the order of weft interlacing.

The Japanese categorize gauze weave into three types:

Ra. The patterned, very complex gauze weaves, usually lozenge designs, woven as early as the seventh century in Japan.

Sha. Plain gauze weave and gauze weaves patterned by areas of plain interlacing or twill floats.

Rō. Fabric woven with bands of plain gauze weave alternating with bands of plain weave.

glossed silk thread. Thread from which the sericin has been removed by boiling it in an alkaline solution. Also called degummed silk thread.

gold-paper thread, flat. In the Edo period, sheets of paper were covered with a paste made from *kuzu*, arrowroot. Lacquer was applied over this, and then gold foil. These sheets were cut into strips by hand and, therefore, are not of uniform width.

In the Meiji period, machinery was used, and the strips were of uniform width. By the late nineteenth century, commercial glues were being used and, when the gold foil wears off, only the paper is visible. On earlier thread, when lacquer was used as the adhesive, the lacquer was visible after the gold leaf wore off.

In 1962 (Showa 36), a pulverized gold amalgam that is self-sticking to the paper and cannot be separated began to be used.

gold-wrapped thread. A thread in which a thread of silk, cotton, or some other fiber forms the core around which strips of flat gold paper are wrapped. *See also* **gold-paper thread, flat.**

gosho mon. Motifs used for *gosho moyō*, palace designs, that pattern garments in the *goshodoki*, Imperial court style. The game of guessing the meaning of these motifs, which referred to poems, classical works, and Nō dramas, was also called *goshodoki*, literally, "the guessing game of the court." The earliest style of this patterning was called *goten mono*, referring to a *daimyo*'s palace, *goten*, not the Imperial palace, *gosho*.

hakama. See "Types of Nō Costumes."

hananoshi. See noshi.

hangiri. See "Types of Nō Costumes."

haori. An informal three-quarter length outer coat, usually lined to the waist (including the sleeves) with a patterned fabric.

happi. See "Types of Nō Costumes."

hitatare. See "Types of Nō Costumes."

hitoe. Literally "one layer." *Hitoe* used as a noun is the name for an unlined silk summer *kosode*. As an adjective, *hitoe* is used to describe a single-layered garment such as an unlined *kariginu*.

hōsōge. A highly stylized, imaginary flower of Buddhist origin, probably modeled originally on the peony.

ikat. *See kasuri.*

iro iri. Literally "with color." A term used to designate a *karaori* costume with red in the ground weave making it an appropriate costume to be worn for the role of a young woman.

iro nashi. Literally "without color." A term used to designate a *karaori* costume without red in the ground weave making it an appropriate costume to be worn for the role of an older woman.

ishidatami. Literally "a stone pavement." A pattern of squares of alternating colors; a checkered pattern.

itajime. A resist-dyeing technique in which the part of the pattern to be dyed is carved into two wooden boards. The design on one board is the mirror image of the design on the other board. On both boards small holes are drilled into the areas to be dyed. The fabric is clamped between the boards and then they are either dipped into a dye bath or the boards are laid flat and the dye is poured into the holes in the top board and drains out of the holes in the bottom board.

Jacquard attachment. An attachment for the draw loom patented by Joseph Marie Jacquard (1752–1834) of Lyons, France, in 1804. The attachment consisted of a series of punched cards, linked together, which fed into a mechanism at the top of a draw loom that eliminated the equipment and work of the draw boy in the lifting of the warp threads and provided a means for individual warp manipulation and for greater patterning possibilities. Japan imported it from Lyons in the Early Meiji period.

kamishimo. Literally "upper and lower." The ceremonial or formal costume of the warrior class in the Edo period. The "upper" was the *kataginu* worn over a *noshime* and the "lower" was the *hakama*. A Kyōgen costume worn for the roles of members of the warrior class.

kanedo. A May fly, a fragile, short-lived insect of the *Ephemeridae* family. Often confused with the dragon fly, *tonbo* or *akatonbo*, of the *Odonata* family.

kanoko shibori. "Fawn spot" wrapped resist-dyeing. A dyeing technique in which a small bit of a fabric is lifted either with the fingers or a needle and then wrapped either with silk or cotton thread. When dyed, the wrapped areas resist the dye, creating small undyed circles with a tiny dyed spot, which was the very top of the wrapped areas and was not covered by the thread. These spots resemble the mottled coat of a young deer, a fawn.

Kanze *mizu*. Literally "Kanze water." A stylized design of horizontal rows of rippling and swirling flowing water. It is thought to have originated in the patterning of the costumes of the Kanze school of Nō drama.

karabana or ***karabana*.** Literally "Chinese flower." This design of a highly stylized, imaginary flower of four or five petals came to Japan from T'ang Dynasty China. There are many variations of this flower that originally may have been modeled after a fruit tree blossom. When the four petals are so stylized that they form a lozenge, it is called *hanabishi*, "lozenge-shaped flower."

***karakusa*.** Literally "Chinese grasses." A design of curving tendrils, sometimes with leaves and flowers, introduced into Japan from T'ang Dynasty China in the eighth century. "Arabesque," another translation of "*karakusa*," is an inaccurate description of these textile designs. Unfortunately, it was chosen rather than "foliage" or "scroll work," two other meanings of *karakusa*.

***karaori* (costume).** *See* "Types of Nō Costumes."

***karaori* (fabric).** The fabric used for the *kosode* worn for the Nō drama roles that require a *karaori* costume. A *karaori* is woven in a warp-faced 2/1 twill weave patterned with long floats of supplementary brocading wefts that resemble needlework stitches. In the Heian period, textiles imported from China were called *karaori*, meaning "Chinese weaving." In the fifteenth and sixteenth centuries, sumptuous textiles imported from Ming Dynasty China were used for Nō costumes, and in time one of these textiles was used exclusively for *karaori kosode*. Shortly after 1578, the weavers of Kyoto were producing *karaori* to imitate the Momoyama period needlework.

***kariginu*.** *See* "Types of Nō Costumes."

***kariginu, awase*.** A *kariginu* with a lining.

***kasumi*.** Literally "mist." Horizontal bands with borders of repeated curving lines, representing trailing mists.

***kasuri*.** A fabric woven in plain weave with the warps or wefts dyed before weaving to create the patterning. Sometimes both warps and wefts are pre-dyed. Also called "ikat." Rung dyeing is a type of *kasuri*.

***katabira*.** An unlined patterned *kosode* made of ramie or hemp worn in the summer.

***kataginu*.** Literally "the silk covering the shoulders." The sleeveless, broad-shouldered "upper" garment of the *kamishimo* worn tucked into the *hakama*, the "lower" garment.

***katamigawari*.** Literally "one side differs from the other." One of the three types of sectional placement of patterning on *kosode*, in which two differently patterned fabrics are used full length on each side of the vertical seams of the *kosode*. Garments were divided in this manner as early as the Heian period.

***katasuso*.** Literally "shoulders and bottom." One of the three types of sectional placement of patterning on *kosode*, in which the patterning appears only from the level of the shoulders to the chest and from knee level to the hemline. The patterned areas of the *kosode* are divided from the unpatterned middle section by either a straight line or a series of curved lines suggestive of trailing mists, *kasumi*.

***kikyō*.** *Platycodon grandiflorum*, the balloon flower. Sometimes confused with the bellflower which is a member of the *Campanula* family.

kimono. Literally "the thing worn." Originally, to the Japanese "kimono" meant simply "clothing," but today "kimono" sometimes is used, often in Roman letters, both as a generic term for all types of *kosode* and as the name for any contemporary garment that in any way resembles a *kosode*. However, the contemporary wearer of these garments uses the proper Japanese name for each garment. *Kosode*, not "kimono," is the generic term used when referring to the kimono-like garments worn in earlier periods.

***kinran*.** A fabric with a monochromatic ground woven in a plain, twill, or satin weave and patterned usually with a supplementary weft of flat gold-paper thread. Sometimes gold-wrapped thread is used as the supplementary patterning weft.

***kitsuke*.** *See* "Types of Nō Costumes."

***kōbone*.** *Nuphar japonicum*, called candock or spatterdock.

***koshi obi*.** A narrow sash used to adjust the length of Nō jackets and coats. It consists of the sash and a patterned band, sometimes fringed, which is suspended from the front of the sash.

***koshimaki* (costume).** *See* "Types of Nō Costumes."

***koshimaki* (style).** A summer style worn by upper-class women of the warrior class. It began in the late Muromachi period when women slipped their arms out of the *uchikake*, allowing the upper part of the garment to fall freely from the waist, where it was held in place by the narrow *obi* worn during that period. Hence, the name *koshimaki*, "waist wrap." In the Edo period, it became the most formal summer style and was worn from April 1st to September 8th. The undergarment was a *katabira*, and the draped *uchikake* was at first red, and later brown or black, *nerinuki* patterned with *takarazukushi* motifs. These *uchikake* were lined with a red plain woven silk called *momi*. In this later period the *uchikake* was suspended at the waist on a thin lacquer bar that passed through a knot at the back of the *obi*. The bar extended on each side of the waist to the edge of the sleeve.

***kosode*.** Literally "small sleeves." The *kosode* is the forerunner of the modern kimono worn by married women. In the Heian period, it was worn as an undergarment by both men and women of court nobility. By the Muromachi period, it had become the outer garment for all classes. The "small sleeves" referred originally to the small opening for the wrist, which distinguished the *kosode* from the *ōsode*, "large sleeves," in which the wrist opening was the full length of the sleeve. In modern times, *kosode* also have "small sleeves" in the sense that they are shorter than those of the *furisode*.

***kosodemono*.** *See* "Types of Nō Costumes."

***kuzu*.** Arrowroot, *Pueraria thunbergiana*, or arrowroot starch.

Kyōgen. Literally "wild words." An interlude of light social comedy or parody between two Nō plays in which the actors use ordinary speech or a dialect and do not wear masks. There is no musical accompaniment.

***maiginu*.** *See* "Types of Nō Costumes."

***matsu kawa bishi*.** Literally "pine-bark lozenges." A stylized motif composed of tiered lozenges based on the patterning that appears on the surface of the bark of the pine tree.

***mawata*.** The silk wadding processed from the cocoons that have been pierced as the moth emerged from the cocoon. The thread cannot be reeled as a continuous filament from a pierced cocoon, but the cocoon can be stretched into a fairly large, flat, thin square of wadding.

mechō. See ōchō.

mizugoromo. See "Types of Nō Costumes."

mon. Japanese family crest. It began as an heraldic emblem in the Heian period. Soon each noble family, the *daimyo*, began to adopt a specific crest. In the feudal period, samurai families adopted a *mon* to identify members of their clan during battles. After the Meiji restoration, the common people were permitted to use a family *mon*.

needlework. A general term which encompasses many techniques employing a needle to embellish a foundation fabric with thread, such as appliquéing, embroidering, pulled thread, and cut and drawn work.

nerinuki. Plain weave silk woven with reeled unglossed warps and reeled glossed (degummed) wefts.

Nishijin. Literally "Western camp." A western area of Kyoto where, since the early sixteenth century, most of the finest patterned silks have been woven. The name refers to the area occupied by one of the armies of the rival groups during the civil strife, known as the Onin wars, 1467–1477. After this devastating strife, some weavers returned to the "Eastern camp," Higashijin, and others to the "Western camp," Nishijin. In 1513, the two groups of weavers were engaged in a struggle over the production of "figured silk," *ayaginu.* The Nishijin group was the victor, and in time the weavers from Higashijin established themselves in the Nishijin area.

nishiki. A generic term for a polychromatic woven patterned silk fabric. In recent times, *nishiki* has been translated as a "brocade," which for most of these fabrics is only a description of its appearance, not the manner in which it was woven. Some of the fabrics called *nishiki* have been given names based on the techniques used in the patterning; the wefts used for the patterning as in *nishiki kinran*; and the places in which they were woven (for example, *Nankin nishiki*, woven in Nanking). As late as 1914, Ezo *nishiki*, with its Chinese patterning of dragons chasing the sacred pearl amidst clouds, was thought to be woven in Ezo (Yezo), the earlier name of Hokkaido and the pattern was thought to be an original Ainu design. This misunderstanding arose because the earliest fabrics with this design were imported from China through the northern ports of Japan. In 1963, "Ezo *nishiki*" was still used as the name for fabrics with this patterning woven on the looms of Nishijin in Kyoto.

noshi. Originally a *noshi* was a bundle of thin strips of dried abalone placed on a gift. Later it became a bundle of colorful bands of cloth tied in an ornamental knot. Then it became a piece of folded paper, *origami*, in which was inserted a strip of dried abalone. If the abalone is replaced by flowers, it is called a *hananoshi.*

nōshi. See "Types of Nō Costumes."

noshime. See "Types of Nō Costumes."

nuihaku. See "Types of Nō Costumes."

obi. The generic term for the sash worn by both men and women. There are many types of *obi*, and each has a specific name.

ōbōshi shibori. See shibori.

ōchō and *mechō*. A male butterfly, *ōchō*, and a female butterfly, *mechō*, made of folded paper, *origami*. During a wedding ceremony, they are placed on the two sake bottles, and the pitcher and the ladle function as symbols that carry a wish for many descendants.

ōguchi. See "Types of Nō Costumes."

ōsodemono. See "Types of Nō Costumes."

plain weave. The simplest interlacing of warp and weft. Each weft passes alternately over and under successive warps. With each passage of the weft, the alternating procedure is reversed.

plain weave, warp-faced, with weft ribs. A plain weave in which the warps are predominant on the face of the weave and conceal wefts, which are larger in diameter, producing a ribbed fabric.

poem papers. The square sheets of fancy paper, *shikishi*, and the rectangular sheets, *tanzaku*, on which poems were written. They were also used for painting a picture.

reeling. The process of unwinding the silk filaments from an unbroken cocoon, during which the filaments are reeled on a slatted cylindrical drum. Additional reelings are necessary to combine the filaments to make a thread strong enough to be used.

rimbō. Also spelled *rinbō.* The Buddhist wheel of power, one of seven treasures given to an ideal king at his enthronement. It destroys enemies of the king and levels the ground before him. The gold wheel is a treasure of the king who rules the four continents of the world. There are also silver, copper, and iron wheels given to kings ruling only three, two, or one continents.

rinzu. See satin damask weave, rinzu.

rung dyeing. See *kasuri.*

safflower. See *benibana.*

samurai. A member of an arms-bearing family permitted to wear two swords but ranking below the *daimyo*, the feudal lords, in the warrior class.

sashinuki. See "Types of Nō Costumes."

satin damask weave. A self-patterned satin weave where the pattern is produced by the juxtaposition of the warp and weft faces of the weave.

satin damask weave, *donsu*. A soft, lustrous, monochromatic patterned satin weave fabric. The warps and wefts are degummed (glossed) and dyed prior to being woven. Usually *donsu* is woven with 4/1 warp-faced satin for the ground weave and 1/4 weft-faced satin for the patterning. Satin damask is reversible with the patterning on one side, the reverse weave structure of the patterning on the other side. Depending upon the angle at which the fabric reflects the light, the warps and wefts appear to differ slightly in color.

satin damask weave, *rinzu*. A soft lustrous, monochromatic patterned satin weave fabric. It is woven with the sericin still in the warps and wefts and is degummed (glossed) and dyed after being woven. Usually *rinzu* is woven in 4/1 or 7/1 warp-faced satin for the ground weave and 1/4 or 1/7 weft-faced satin weave for the patterning. The fabric is reversible. The scheme of the patterning of *rinzu* differs from satin damask weave, *donsu*, in that *rinzu* has a more equal balance between the amount of space allotted to the ground weave and that occupied by the patterning.

satin stitches. These are two basic types of stitches used in various ways to create a desired texture or artistic effect. The earliest, using the least thread, is the surface or single layer satin stitch, *hira nui*. When this stitch is worked, the needle is brought again to the surface of the fabric close to where it had completed the surface stitch. Consequently, the stitches on the reverse side are very small and do not cover the motif being embroidered. This single layer satin stitch was used on Momoyama-period needlework pieces. In the Edo period, the satin stitch used most often in Western needlework began to be used. In this case the thread is carried across the motif on the reverse side and brought to the surface again some distance from where the earlier stitch had been completed. If carefully worked, the needlework appears exactly the same on both sides of the fabric. There are numerous effects that can be created with satin stitches, and each has a specific name.

satin weave, *shusu*. A simple float weave requiring a minimum of five warp and weft groups where warps float over a minimum of four wefts, are never bound by more than one weft, and diagonal alignment of floats is prevented by maintaining at least one intervening warp between binding points on successive wefts.

sayagata. This is a diaper pattern with a fret of interlocking swastikas. Against this fret may be superimposed at regular intervals flowers or lucky symbols. About 1570 in Kyoto, a fine twill weave in this pattern was woven for the first time. The Portuguese called this twill weave *saia*, and in time it came to be known as *sayagata*, literally "twill pattern," combining the Portuguese work, "*saia*" with the Japanese word "*gata*," i.e., "hata."

sei-ga-ha. An imbricated design of overlapping semicircles representing the waves of the ocean.

sericin. A gummy substance that glues together the filaments in a cocoon.

The Seven Plants of Autumn, *Aki no nanakusa*. Literally "The Seven Grasses of Autumn." These "Autumn Grasses," *Akikusa*, also include flowering plants and weeds. A poem in the *Manyōshū*, c. 730, mentions "the flowers of seven kinds" including bush clover, eulalia, arrowroot, valerian, fringed pink, agrimony, and *asagao*, a morning flower, which in more recent times has come to mean the morning glory. Over the centuries, the list has varied. Often the balloon flower and chrysanthemum are included among the autumn "grasses."

shibori. A resist-dyeing technique in which a fabric is gathered or compressed by a wrapped or stitched thread prior to dyeing to prevent these areas from taking dye. If necessary, an additional protective resist can be applied before dyeing. In *ōbōshi shibori*, a fabric is gathered together with the fingers against a circular disk inserted beneath the fabric, and these gathers are held in place by wrapping a string around the disk. The cloth not to be dyed is resisted by covering it with bamboo husks.

shippō. A Buddhist term meaning "seven treasures," or "seven kinds of precious stones." There are numerous versions of this pattern of interlocking circles. The most common form is a series of interlocking circles in which a small concave-sided square is formed wherever four circles interlock. Often a stylized flower is in this lozenge.

shusu. See **satin weave, *shusu*.**

sobatsugi. See "Types of Nō Costumes."

sōmoyō. A graphic presentation of a single design or theme for the patterning of the entire costume.

spinning. The process of drawing out short fibers and twisting them together into a continuous strand either by hand or machine.

stem stitch. A linear stitch moving forward on the front of the cloth and partway back on the underside of the cloth. The needle emerges consistently on either the right or the left of the float. Sometimes called "outline stitch."

sumi **ink.** A black ink made of pine-wood charcoal or lamp soot mixed with a gum-like substance soluble in water.

suō. See "Types of Nō Costumes."

supplementary weft floats. *See* **weft floats, supplementary.**

surihaku. See "Types of Nō Costumes."

surihitta. A stenciled imitation of the *shibori* technique called *hitta* in which small square motifs with a small dot of color in the center cover a specific area. These center dots form a line, the angle of which is the same as the line that divides a square into two 45° triangles. It began to be used from the third year of the Tenna era, 1683, when sumptuary laws forbade the use of *hitta*.

susuki, **eulalia.** *Miscanthus sinensis*, a tall ornamental grass. The ear or plume, the seed pod, is called *obana*.

tachibana. Citrus *tachibana*, a mandarin orange, a tangerine. The *Manyōshū* has a poem dated 749 calling this the "Timeless Fragrant Fruit" brought to Japan in ancient times from the "Land of Eternity."

tanzaku. See **poem papers.**

tatewaku. A yūsoku motif of opposed vertical serpentine lines in which the lines used in pairs are mirror images, one of the other.

tessen. Clematis, a genus that includes over two hundred species of flowering deciduous vines.

thread, twist of. The twist of a thread is described depending upon how the spiral of the twist conforms either to the slant of the central portion of the letter "S" or the letter "Z," i.e., S-twisted or Z-twisted.

thread, untwisted. Thread that shows no visible twist, such as extremely long silk filaments. Technically, filaments undergo some twisting in the throwing process that unites the filaments to make a thread usable for weaving.

tie-dyeing. *See* **shibori.**

twill weave. A simple float weave requiring a minimum of three warp and weft groups where warps are bound on successive wefts producing a diagonal alignment of binding points.

twist of thread. *See* **thread, twist of.**

ubugi. Literally "baby clothes." *Ubugi*, however, is the word used for the *kosode* in which the baby will be carried when introduced to the god of the local shrine. This can vary in size and patterning from a small baby-size *kosode* to a full-size *kosode*, which the child will wear later in life. An *ubugi* has padding and cords or bands inside to wrap around the baby to hold the garment in place.

uchikake. A formal outer *kosode* worn as a coat without a sash, *obi*, over a *kosode* belted with an *obi*.

unglossed silk thread. Silk thread which still contains its sericin.

untwisted thread. *See* **thread, untwisted.**

warp. The longitudinal threads stretched on a loom before weaving.

warp-faced weave. A weave in which the warp predominates on the face of the fabric, more or less concealing the weft.

warp float. *See* **float** or **floats.**

weft. The transverse threads inserted over and under the warps during the process of weaving.

weft floats, supplementary. *See* **float** or **floats** and **wefts, supplementary.**

wefts, supplementary brocading. Weft sets additional to those that form the ground weave, which produce the pattern. Supplementary brocading wefts are inserted only in those areas of the weave where patterning is required.

wefts, supplementary patterning. Weft sets, additional to those that form the ground weave, which produce the pattern. Supplementary patterning wefts extend the full width of the fabric and are visible on the face of the weave only as required by the pattern.

Yatsuhashi. Literally "eight bridges." The plank bridge made in eight sections zigzagging across a marsh filled with blooming iris refers to a chapter in the *Ise Monogatari* in which Ariwara Narihira comes upon this scene writing a poem to his wife lamenting his arduous trip and expressing his longing for her.

Yezo *nishiki* *See* **nishiki.**

yogi. A padded coverlet made like a *kosode* used as bedding.

yuki mochi yanagi. This motif of willow branches laden with snow was a very popular design used on sixteenth-century textiles of the Momoyama period. The resiliency of the snow-laden branches was symbolic of masculine strength tempered with the feminine tenderness associated with the gentle manner in which willow branches yield to the wind.

yūsoku **patterns.** Literally patterns originating in "ancient court and military practices." Originally *yūsoku* meant "learned" or "erudite," referring to the formal customs and practices of the court in the middle Heian period. Since textile designs of the period had to conform to the prescribed aesthetics of *yūsoku*, they became stylized motifs, with many prescribed variations. They have come to represent the taste of the highly venerated Heian period. The many variations often were indicative of rank and, therefore, *yūsoku* patterns have been used for court costumes up until the present time.

yuzen. A very involved process of paste resist-dyeing in which a rice-paste resist is squeezed from a cone by hand onto a white fabric, creating linear designs as well as outlining the pattern areas to be painted with dyes and further resisted with additional rice paste before the entire fabric is dyed. To create a yuzen dyed garment, the fabric is subjected to the following fifteen processes:

1. The fabric is washed.
2. The fabric is steamed to smooth it and to make it a uniform width.
3. The fabric widths are loosely sewn together so that the pattern can be adjusted to the seam allowances, after which the stitching is taken out.
4. The outlines of the patterning are painted on the fabric with a blue extract of *aobana*, var. *Hortensis Makino*, that will disappear when the fabric is washed.
5. The outlines of the patterning are covered with a rice paste resist. When this paste is applied in very fine lines that become a part of the patterning, the yuzen is called *itome yuzen.*

6. The fabric is brushed with a white soybean extract made by dissolving a ground soybean mash in water. It prevents the dyes from running and is essential for the setting of the dyes in Step 8.
7. The motifs in the patterned areas outlined by the resist paste in Step 5 are painted with dyes.
8. The fabric is steamed to set the dyes.
9. The patterned areas are covered with a thick layer of rice paste.
10. The entire fabric is brushed with the white soybean extract to assure an evenly colored background.
11. The dye for the background is brushed over the entire surface of the fabric.
12. The fabric is steamed to set the background dye.
13. All the paste and excess dye is washed out of the fabric.
14. The fabric is steamed to smooth it and make it a uniform width.
15. The fabric is sewn into a garment.

Isoda Koryūsai (Japanese, active 1766–1788). *Oiran Tamazusa no Ieta-ya (Courtesan Tamazusa of House of Ieta)*, c. 1775. From the series *Hinagata Wakana no Hatsu Moyō (New Designs as Fresh as Young Leaves)*. Woodblock print; 37.8 x 25.4 cm. The Art Institute of Chicago, Clarence Buckingham Collection of Japanese Prints (1925.2231).

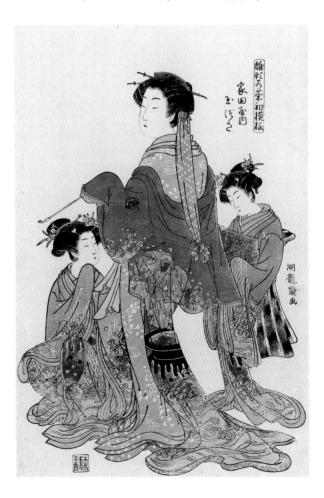

Notes

BETHE, "The Use of Costumes in Nō Drama," pp. 6–19.

1. Kentarō Sanari, *Yōkyoku taikan (Anthology of Nō Plays)*, vol. 1 (Tokyo, 1982), pp. 156–68. For a translation of *Aoinoue*, see Arthur Waley, ed., *The Noh Plays of Japan* (New York, 1957), pp. 179–89. In the variant performance of *Aoinoue* known as *Mumyōnoinori*, a white kimono represents Lady Aoi.

2. Sanari (note 1), vol. 1, p. 386. The Japanese texts of Nō plays are drawn from this edition. All translations in this essay are my own. I have discussed the use of the hunter's hat as a prop in *Dance in the Noh Theater* (Cornell University East Asia Papers, no. 29), vol. 1 (Ithaca, N.Y., 1982), pp. 91–95. For a translation of the play *Utō*, see "Birds of Sorrow," in Donald Keene, ed., *Anthology of Japanese Literature* (Harmondsworth, 1968), pp. 263–74.

3. Sanari (note 1), vol. 4, p. 2489. A good translation of *Hagoromo* is forthcoming in Royall Tyler, ed., *Japanese Nō Dramas* (London, 1992).

4. Sanari (note 1), vol. 1, p. 87. For a translation of *Ataka*, see Nippon Gakujitsu Shinkōkai, ed., *Japanese Noh Drama*, vol. 3 (Tokyo, 1960), pp. 149–72.

5. Sanari (note 1), vol. 1, p. 91.

6. Hiroshi Koyama, *Kyōgenshūge (Collection of Kyōgen Plays)*, vol. 2, in *Nihon bungaku taikei (Anthology of Japanese Literature)*, vol. 43 (Tokyo, 1970), pp. 180–86.

7. Sanari (note 1), vol. 3, p. 1727. For a translation of *Sotoba Komachi*, see Nippon Gakujitsu Shinkōkai (note 4), vol. 3, pp. 77–94. The version quoted here is inspired by an unpublished translation by Gus Held. In the Japanese poetic tradition, the sleeve is the primary receptacle for tears. This image is represented onstage by an actor raising his hand with his outstretched fingers pointing up until they shade his forehead, while the sleeve of his robe covers his eyes.

8. Sanari (note 1), vol. 3, p. 1729.

9. Ibid., vol. 4, p. 2716. For a translation of *Futari Shizuka*, see Chifumi Shimazaki, *The Noh, Vol. III: Woman Noh, Book 3* (Tokyo, 1981), pp. 32–63.

10. Sanari (note 1), vol. 4, p. 2717–18. The fabric is *seigo-o*, which is woven with glossed silk wefts, and sometimes warps, as well. It is commonly used for women's red *hakama*. *Suikan* are broad-sleeved, round-necked courtier's cloaks, similar to *kariginu* (see pl. 18, as well as cat. no. 16, for The Art Institute of Chicago's *kariginu*).

11. In modern performances of *Futari Shizuka*, both Shizuka and the shrine girl are dressed in similar *chōken*. But an eighteenth-century illustration of the play in the Date Collection shows one character dressed in a white *chōken*, and the other in a green *chōken*.

12. Sanari (note 1), vol. 4, p. 2721.

13. Sanari (note 1), vol. 5, pp. 2822–38. *Matsukaze* is translated by Royall Tyler in Donald Keene, ed., *Twenty Plays of the Nō Theater* (New York, 1970), pp. 17–34; an additional translation will appear in Tyler (note 3).

14. Sanari (note 1), vol. 5, pp. 3411–12. The phrase "Man of Long Ago" is an epithet for Narihira used in the *Tales of Ise*. For a translation of *Izutsu*, see Thomas Hare, *Zeami's Style: The Noh Plays of Zeami Motokiyo* (Stanford, Calif., 1986), pp. 135–53.

15. Sanari (note 1), vol. 1, p. 621. *Kakitsubata* is translated by Susan Klein in Karen Brazell, ed., *Twelve Plays of the Noh and Kyōgen Theaters* (Cornell University East Asia Papers, no. 50) (Ithaca, N.Y., 1988), pp. 63–80.

16. *Chōken* are unlined; therefore, the *chōken* belonging to the Art Institute must have been resewn. See pls. 12 and 14, cat. nos. 10–11.

17. Kitamura Tetsurō, *Nō shōzoku (Nō Costumes)*, in *Nihon no bijutsu*, no. 46 (Tokyo, 1970), pp. 25–44.

18. Sanari (note 1), vol. 5, p. 2983. *Miwa* is translated by Monica Bethe in Brazell (note 15), pp. 23–38.

19. Sanari (note 1), vol. 2, pp. 975–88. For a translation of *Kureha*, see Tyler (note 3).

20. Sanari (note 1), vol. 1, p. 213.

21. Ibid., vol. 2, pp. 831–34. For a translation of *Kinuta*, see Tyler (note 3).

22. Sanari (note 1), vol. 2, p. 772. In a standard performance, the pants worn by the performers are the all-purpose, broadly divided skirts with bulging back known as *ōguchi*. In some performances of *Sotoba Komachi*, however, these skirts can be replaced by the courtier's ankle-bound *sashinuki*, which would then illustrate not Captain Fukakusa's hellish torment, but his rank among the nobility.

23. Sanari (note 1), vol. 5, p. 3179. For a translation and discussion of this scene in *Yamamba*, see Monica Bethe and Karen Brazell, *Nō as Performance: An Analysis of the Kuse Scene of Yamamba* (Cornell University East Asia Papers, no. 16) (Ithaca, N.Y., 1978). For a translation of *Yamamba* in its entirety, see Tyler (note 3).

24. Sanari (note 1), vol. 5, p. 3183. The performance version described here is a Kanze school variant known as *Shirogashira (White Headpiece)*, and can be viewed in the videotape *Yamamba Act II* available through the East Asia Papers, Cornell University.

HAYS and HAYS, "Nō Drama Costumes and Other Japanese Costumes in The Art Institute of Chicago," pp. 20–36.

We wish to express our appreciation for the warm hospitality and invaluable assistance of Mrs. Christa C. Thurman and her staff in the Department of Textiles at The Art Institute of Chicago, especially Cynthia J. Castañeda, Lorna Ann Filippini, and Eva-Maria J. Schuchardt. We are grateful for the assistance of Mr. James Ulak, Associate Curator of Japanese Art at the Art Institute.

We are especially thankful for the assistance given to us by Akihiko Takemura, Keiko Kobayashi, Akira Yamaguchi, and Monica Bethe, who answered many questions while we were in Kyoto, and shared with us information that is available only from scholars who have spent years researching Japanese textiles and costumes.

1. William K. Bunce, ed., *Religions in Japan* (Rutland, Vt., 1959), pp. 3, 105.

2. Earl Miner with Hiroko Odagiri and Robert E. Morrell, *The Princeton Companion to Classical Japanese Literature* (Princeton, N.J., 1985), pp. 185–86, 209–10.

3. Akihiko Takemura, *Fukusa, Japanese Gift-Covers* (Tokyo, 1991), p. 134. The symbolic relationship between the traditional Japanese patterning on *fukusa* and the emotion expressed by the giver of the gift is carefully analyzed in this definitive book on *fukusa*.

4. Ken Kirihata, "Textile Designs of the Edo Period: The Japanese Style of Beauty," in Akihiko Takemura, *Fukusa, the Gift-Covers: The Beauty of Japanese Exchanging Gifts*, exh. cat. (Tokyo, 1991), p. 7. This is the catalogue published for an exhibition of the Dennosuki Miyai Fukusa Collection held in Kyoto and Tokyo in 1991.

5. Murasaki Shikibu, *Genji Monogatari*, trans. Kencho Suematsu (Tokyo, 1974), p. 45.

6. Donald L. Keene, *Nō: The Classical Theatre of Japan* (Tokyo, 1970), p. 22.

7. Ibid., p. 25.

8. Arthur Waley, *The Nō Plays of Japan* (London, 1954), p. 15.

9. Ibid., p. 17.

10. Ken Kirihata, "Special Features of Noh Costumes," in Yamaguchi Noh Costume Research Center, *The World of Noh Costumes* (Kyoto, 1989), p. 33.

11. The "stripping" donations were of two types. The garments could be kept and used as costumes in the Nō drama, or the donor would later buy back the garment he "stripped off," and this money would be used to commission a new Nō robe. Conversation with Akira Yamaguchi, Kyoto, September 1991.

12. Akira Yamaguchi, "Noh Costumes of the Middle and Late Edo Period," in Yamaguchi Noh Costume Research Center (note 10), p. 43.

13. Daiji Maruoka and Tatsuo Yoshikoshi, *Noh*, 8th ed., trans. Don Kenny (Osaka, 1980), p. 109.

14. Keene (note 6), p. 73.

15. Maruoka and Yoshikoshi (note 13), p. 109.

16. Monica Bethe, "Colors in Noh Costumes," in Yamaguchi Noh Costume Research Center (note 10), p. 63.

17. See Iwao Nagasaki, "Discovery of Kimono, The Hidden Treasure in America, (3) The Art Institute of Chicago" (in Japanese and English), *The Quarterly Magazine of Beautiful Kimono* (in Japanese) 151 (Mar. 1990), p. 171. Ten of the Art Institute's Nō costumes and six of its *kosode* are reproduced in color in this article.

18. Kirihata (note 10), pp. 33–34.

19. This analysis was done with the assistance of Akihiko Takemura using an enlargement of a photograph of the patterning of the back of the *nuihaku* Nō costume. The *kosode* photograph was cut along the back seam into two lengths of "fabric." These were accordian-pleated to conform to the folding used in the *itajime* dyeing process.

20. Yamaguchi (note 12), p. 43.

21. The textile analysis of the Momoyama *nuihaku* Nō costume was done by Lorna Ann Filippini, Associate Conservator in the Department of Textiles at The Art Institute of Chicago. She also did an analysis for each of the garments discussed in this article and described in the catalogue.

22. Nagasaki (note 17), p. 175.

23. Eva-Maria Schuchardt, Departmental Scientist in the Department of Textiles at The Art Institute of Chicago, has analyzed this thread: "It has a cotton core around which is wound a thin gold or gold alloy strip on amber-colored adhesive over a fibrous backing."

24. Yamaguchi (note 12), p. 43. First an arrowroot starch was spread over the paper, then lacquer was spread over the paste and the gold foil was applied.

25. These *atsuita karaori* fabrics are firm because they have an all-over background pattern of supplementary wefts that are closely bound. Over this background pattern, the long supplementary brocading wefts create a patterning that uses large, dominant motifs.

26. Tokyo National Museum, *Noh and Kyōgen Play Costumes*, exh. cat. (Tokyo, 1987), p. 5.

27. Tokyo National Museum, *Kosode Dress* (Tokyo, 1983), p. vi. This is one of the museum's fully illustrated catalogues of its textile holdings.

28. Tomoyuki Yamanobe, "Foreword," in Takemura (note 3), p. 7.

29. Three *aoi* leaves were the crest, *mon*, of the Tokugawa shogun, and crests with variations of the leaves of the *aoi* could be used only by the various branches of the Tokugawa family.

30. Nagasaki (note 17), p. 185.

31. P. W. Gaddum, *Silk, How and Where It Is Produced* (Macclesfield, 1979), p. 52.

32. Helen Benton Minnich, in collaboration with Shojiro Nomura, *Japanese Costume and the Makers of Its Elegant Tradition* (Rutland, Vt., 1963), pp. 195–96.

33. Shojiro Nomura, *An Historical Sketch of Nishiki and Kinran Brocades, with a Catalog* (Boston, 1914), p. 35.

34. Ibid., p. 37.

ULAK, "Utamaro's Views of Sericulture," pp. 73–85.

1. Kitagawa Utamaro's *Joshoku kaiko tewaza gusa* (c. 1802), a set of twelve color woodblock prints featuring women at work in the various stages of the sericulture process, was acquired from Yamanaka and Company by Kate Buckingham in 1914, the year after her brother's death, and was given to The Art Institute of Chicago in 1925.

2. Shibusawa Keizō, *Nihon Joshoku Seikatsu Eihiki* (Tokyo, 1984), vol. 3, p. 104.

3. Tokugawa Yoshinobu et al., *Ishiyama-dera Engi*, vol. 18, from *Nihon E-maki Taisei*, ed. Komatsu Shigemi, 26 vols. (Tokyo, 1978).

4. Chiba Jōryū et al., *Boki Ekotoba*, vol. 4, from *Zoku Nihon E-Maki Taisei*, 20 vols. (Tokyo, 1985).

5. Kawahara Yoshio et al., *Taima Mandara Engi, Chigo Kannon Engi*, vol. 24, from *Nihon E-maki Taisei* (note 3).

6. Yamamoto Yuiitsu, "Tōhoku-in to Tsurugaoka Hōjō-e: Kamakura ki shoku-nin utaawase no seiritsu," *Kobijutsu* 74 (Apr. 1985).

7. Takeda Tsuneo et al., *Fūzoku: Rakuchu-Rakugai*, vol. 11, from *Nihon Byobu-e Shusei*, 17 vols. (Tokyo, 1982).

8. Sherman Lee et al., *Eight Dynasties of Chinese Painting: The Collections of the Nelson Gallery-Atkins Museum, Kansas City, and The Cleveland Museum of Art*, exh. cat. (Cleveland, 1980), pp. 78–90.

9. Ibid.

10. Dieter Kuhn, *Science and Civilization in China, Volume 5: Chemistry and Chemical Technology, Part 9: Textile Technology: Spinning and Reeling*, ed. Joseph Needham (London, 1988), pp. 349–51.

11. J. Hillier, *Utamaro: Colour Prints and Paintings* (London, 1961).

12. Narazaki Muneshige, *Kitagawa Utamaro*, from *Zaigai hiho* (Tokyo, 1973).

13. Suzuki Harunobu (1724–1770) is an example of an artist who used this formulaic approach in portraying silk-making (see fig. 1).

14. Katsukawa Shunshō produced a series entitled *Kaiko yashinai gusa* in 1772. Of this series, impressions of the sixth and eleventh stages (i.e., "forming cocoons" and "weaving") are in the Art Institute's collection (accession nos. 1961.200 and 1960.201; Gift of Chester W. Wright).

15. Katsukawa Shunshō and Kitao Shigemasa, *Sanyo Zue, E-bon Takara no itosuji* (Edo, 1786).

16. Laurence Binyon, *A Catalogue of Japanese and Chinese Woodcuts Preserved in the Sub-Department of Oriental Prints and Drawings in the British Museum* (London, 1916), pp. 219–21.

17. See Muneshige (note 12), supp. vol., figs. 149–60, n. pag. The page layout of images suggests that Utamaro's sericulture series can also be interpreted as three groups of four each, rather than the more common grouping of four triptychs.

SIFFERT, "*Hinagata Bon*: The Art Institute of Chicago Collection of Kimono Pattern Books," pp. 86–94.

1. Kenji Toda, *Descriptive Catalogue of Japanese and Chinese Illustrated Books in the Ryerson Library of The Art Institute of Chicago* (Chicago, 1931).

2. The *hinagata bon* (pattern books) of the Meiji era in the Art Institute's collection have been catalogued in Cheryl Boettcher, "The Kimono Imagined," *Occasional Papers* (University of Illinois Graduate School of Library and Information Science), no. 180 (Nov. 1987).

3. Jack Hillier, *The Art of the Japanese Book* (London, 1987), pp. 112–13.

4. Hillier (note 3), chap. 8 ("Kimono Pattern Books of the Seventeenth Century").

5. Louise Norton Brown, *Block Printing and Book Illustration in Japan* (New York, 1924), p. 203.

6. Christie's, New York, *The Donald and Mary Hyde Collection of Japanese Books and Manuscripts* (Oct. 7, 1988: lot 102).

7. Richard Lane, *Images from the Floating World: The Japanese Print* (New York, 1978), pp. 44–46.

8. See also Hillier (note 3), pp 112–13. See p. 114, pl. 63, for an illustration from another copy of Moronobu's book.

9. For additional information on this work, see Matthi Forrer, *Hokusai*, with text by Edmond de Goncourt (New York, 1988), p. 250, pls. 284–85.

10. See Hillier (note 3), p. 160, and p. 162, pl. 111. The book reproduced in Hillier is in the collection of the Art Institute. There is no standard translation for titles of older Japanese books; Hillier translates this title as *A Comparison of Thirty-Two Different Types*.

Isoda Koryūsai (Japanese, active 1766–1788). *Ukifune no Kane-ya* (*Ukifune of House of Kane*), c. 1778. From the series *Hinagata Wakana no Hatsu Moyō* (*New Designs as Fresh as Young Leaves*). Woodblock print; 37.6 x 24.9 cm. The Art Institute of Chicago, Clarence Buckingham Collection of Japanese Prints (1939.2174).